MORE
LITURGIES
for
Post-Primary
Schools

Brendan Quinlivan

VERITAS

Published 2003 by
Veritas Publications
7/8 Lower Abbey Street
Dublin 1
Ireland

Email publications@veritas.ie
Website www.veritas.ie

Text © Brendan Quinlivan, 2003
Music suggestions © Geraldine Bradley, 2003

ISBN 1 85390 790 1

A catalogue record for this book is available from the British Library.

Veritas books are printed on paper made from the wood pulp of managed forests. For every tree felled, at least one tree is planted, thereby renewing natural resources.

Cover design by Niamh McGarry
Printed in the Republic of Ireland by Criterion Press

'Teach us to Live' by Helen Steiner Rice: used with permission of the Helen Steiner Rice Foundation, Cincinnati, Ohio.
'The Guardian' and 'Unforgiveness' by Allison Chambers Coxsey © 1995 (www.allisonsheart.com); used with permission.
'I'm Free' by Linda Jo Jackson from www.september11-tribute.org.

CONTENTS

INTRODUCTION

It sometimes strikes me that there is an increasing movement in society to privatise the notion of religion. It happens when people reduce faith to being simply about an individual's relationship with God. The truth is that unless our religion has a social or communitarian dimension it is incomplete. This privatisation of religion is also to be seen in the fact that many of our sacraments are celebrated before invited guests alone. It is very possible that many of our people will not have been at a baptism or confirmation apart from their own.

As educators and people responsible for the spiritual formation we are challenged to give our students an experience of religious practice through the liturgy. Since the first book was published many schools have introduced religious education as an exam subject. Religious knowledge without religious experience is also incomplete. Using liturgy creatively will help our students to internalise and experience the knowledge that they have been taught.

I believe that effective liturgy can create a sense of empathy within us leading to an open dialogue with the people of our own time. Christianity is not just a call to relationship with God, but also a call to enter into a just and social relationship with others. Religious truth is never abstract and concept without vision is blind. Liturgy gives us the opportunity to concretise our religious truth and give reality to our concepts.

By means of liturgy the Church proclaimes the liberating mission of Christ. Our spirituality needs to be embodied or it can become buried in personal piety, never being seen or heard above the distractions of modern living. As religious educators we need all the help we can get to create liturgies that embody the spiritual lives of our students. I hope that these liturgies will help you in your work and prompt your own creativity to inspire your students.

Brendan Quinlivan

A NOTE ON THE MUSIC

As a religion teacher and choir director, it was very rewarding and satisfying to receive the positive feedback on *Liturgies for Post-Primary Schools*. Music enhances all aspects of our lives, and as such it should be appreciated, shared and passed on to the next generation. We should not be overly critical of the music in school liturgies, if music can help our students participate and relate in any way to the liturgies, then surely that should be the primary focus of the music. Again in this book, I have tried to suggest music that is accessible, easily learnt, and is not dependent on, but can be enhanced by, the presence of exceptional musical talent in the school.

Geraldine Bradley

Geraldine Bradley is a full time religion teacher in Colaiste Mhuire, Ennis, Co. Clare. She is also a regular presenter of Beyond Belief, *a religious affairs program broadcast every Sunday on Clare FM.*

OPENING OF THE SCHOOL YEAR

LITURGY FOR FIRST YEAR STUDENTS

Scripture texts and music suggestions can be found in the Appendix

If the budget will allow, students could receive a religious gift (e.g. a medal, cross, prayer card) as they begin their time in the secondary school. Giving them something to take away means that the memory and merits of this time of prayer together are carried into the future.

INTRODUCTION

We gather in prayer at the beginning of this new school year. This is a time of great change as we move from primary to secondary school. We may be afraid or anxious of what lies ahead or we may be confident and glad to be here. It is important to remember that no matter how we feel, God is with us as we take this step. We ask God's help with our study, our friendships, our sports, our hobbies, and with everything that is part of school life.

PENITENTIAL RITE

1.   You have come to give us life and love.
   Lord have mercy.

2.   You have come to give us truth and wisdom.
   Christ have mercy.

3.   You have come to give us confidence and hope.
   Lord have mercy.

OPENING PRAYER

God of Love, you watch over and protect all your children. Bless us as we begin this new part of our education. Protect us from all worry and anxiety. Help us in our work and in our friendships. We ask this through Christ our Lord. Amen.

FIRST READING   Phillippians 4:4–9

RESPONSORIAL PSALM

Psalm 34
Response: I will bless the Lord at all times.

GOSPEL

Mark 4:35–41
Jesus calms the storm.

PRAYERS OF INTERCESSION

CELEBRANT   Let us turn in prayer to God asking him for those gifts that will help us as we begin our time in this school.

FIRST YEAR
STUDENT   Loving God, give us the gift of hope so that we can face the future with confidence.

Lord hear us.

SENIOR STUDENT   Eternal Father, give to these new students the gift of friendship so that they will have the help and support they need.

Lord hear us.

TEACHER   Heavenly Father, give to us the gift of wisdom, so that we may grow in knowledge and respect for the world we live in.

Lord hear us.

PRINCIPAL /YEAR HEAD	God of Justice, give the gift of your protection to all your children who make up this school community.
	Lord hear us.
CHAPLAIN /CATECHIST	Ever-living God, grant to all of us the gift of faith so that it may sustain us in times of trial and difficulty.
	Lord hear us.
PARENT	Faithful God, fill each and every one of us with the gift of your love so that this community may be a better place because we are in it.
	Lord hear us.
CELEBRANT	Help us, gracious God, to use wisely and well the gifts you shower on us all. May all we do in this school be in the service of love and goodness. We ask this through Christ Our Lord. Amen.

PRAYER OVER THE GIFTS

Almighty Father, accept the gifts we offer you. They are signs to us of your goodness and generosity. May we all grow in that same spirit of generous love. We ask this through Christ our Lord. Amen.

POST-COMMUNION REFLECTION

THE GUARDIAN

An angel was assigned to you,
On the day you were born;
It watched you as a slumbering babe,
And kept you safe from harm.
It followed every childhood step,
Then guarded you as you grew;

The dangers that you never saw,
God and your angel knew.
For the Father gave the angel,
A mission to fulfil;
To keep and guard you every step,
Was the Heavenly Father's will.
To gently guide you on your path,
To stand and do battle for you;
A constant, holy companion,
Until life's journey is through.
An angel was assigned to you,
On the day that you were born;
A Guardian sent to walk with you,
To keep you safe from harm.

Allison Chamber Coxsey

CONCLUDING PRAYER

Lord our God, bless these young people as they begin their time together in secondary school. Guide all those who care for them and fill all your children with a spirit of love and joy.

We ask this through Christ our Lord. Amen

OPENING OF THE SCHOOL YEAR

A LITURGY FOR EXAM CLASSES

Scripture texts and music suggestions can be found in the Appendix

Students could be given a prayer card that they can keep and use as a source of prayer during the exam year. This should be laminated if possible as it is our hope it will be used often.

INTRODUCTION

We come together in prayer for the first time in this challenging year. We turn to God for his help in the future we face. There are many times in the year ahead when we will struggle with our studies and other aspects of our lives. Help us to remember that there are many people there to help us with their care and support. Give us also the insight to see when our friends need our help and support.

O God of Wisdom,
I thank you for the gift of learning and knowledge,
I ask you to illuminate my mind and heart.
Let your Holy Spirit be with me as I prepare for exams,
guiding my studies and giving me insight.
Grant me the strength to handle the pressure,
the confidence to feel secure in my knowledge,
the ability to keep perspective
and the peace of mind I need.
In the name of Jesus the Lord. Amen.

talents ?

PENITENTIAL RITE

1.   You came into the world to show God's love and care.
     Lord have mercy.

2.   You strengthen us by your care and protection.
     Christ have mercy.

3.   You give us hope and courage by your constant presence.
     Lord have mercy.

OPENING PRAYER

Lord God and giver of life, as we come to a new year in school, we know that you are the one who binds us together. Strengthen us as we face the future. Give us the courage we need to face the challenges ahead. May we have the wisdom to study sensibility this year and the confidence to give of our best. We ask this through Christ our Lord. Amen.

FIRST READING   Isaiah 55:6–9

RESPONSORIAL PSALM

            Psalm 20
            Response: The Lord answers in the day of trouble.

GOSPEL   Luke 11:9–13

PRAYERS OF INTERCESSION

Celebrant   Lord Jesus, you promised us that if we ask, we will receive. With confidence in that promise we now turn to you to ask for the gifts and graces that will help us in this year ahead.

1.   Gracious Lord, we seek the gift of perseverance. Sustain us when we falter. Keep us faithful to our studies and our relationship with you.

   Lord hear us.

2.   Gracious Lord, we seek the gift of wisdom. Enlighten our minds and help us to grow in knowledge.

   Lord hear us.

3.   Gracious Lord, we seek the gift of humour. Help us to always keep things in perspective. Give us a healthy balance in our lives.

   Lord hear us.

4.   Gracious Lord, we seek the gift of hope. Help us to see beyond this year of examination. Guide us as we try to follow your ways.

   Lord hear us.

5.   Gracious Lord, we seek the gift of judgement. Show us the way as we make important choices this year. Guide us in the decisions we make.

   Lord hear us.

6.   Gracious Lord, we seek the gift of love. Remind us that when all else passes only love remains. Strengthen us in this year ahead and through all our difficulties keep us alive in your love.

   Lord hear us.

Celebrant   Ever-loving God, these are the prayers of your children at this important time of their lives. Bless them with your love and grant all their needs through Christ our Lord. Amen.

PRAYER OVER THE GIFTS

Creator of the Universe, accept the gifts we offer you, they are the gifts of our hearts. Make us joyful in your love for us and confidence in your loving care. We ask this through Christ our Lord. Amen.

POST COMMUNION REFLECTION

PRAYER OF ARCHBISHOP OSCAR ROMERO

We are workers. It helps now and then to step back and take the long view. The kingdom is not only beyond our efforts, it is even beyond our vision.

This is what we are about. We plant the seeds that one day will grow. We water the seeds that are already plants, knowing that they hold future promise. We lay foundations that will need future development. We provide yeast that produces effect beyond our capabilities.

We cannot do everything and there is a sense of liberation in realising that. This enables us to do something and do it very well. It may be incomplete but it is a beginning, a step along the way, an opportunity for the Lord's grace to enter and do the rest. We may never see the end results, but that is the difference between the master builder and the worker.

We are workers, not master-builders, ministers not messiahs. We are prophets of a future not our own.

Archbishop Oscar Romero was Bishop of San Salvador. He was a great defender of the poor. He constantly spoke out for justice and against violence. Like Christ he called both rich and poor to forgiveness and conversion. He was assassinated as he celebrated mass on 24 March 1980. The blood of martyrs is the seed of Christians.

CONCLUDING PRAYER

Lord our God, bless us as we begin this examination year together. Strengthened by the power (of this Eucharist) and your loving presence in our lives may we face the future with courage and hope. We ask this through Christ our Lord. Amen.

A SERVICE OF PRAYER
FOR TEACHERS

Scripture texts and music suggestions can be found in the Appendix

Sometimes the catechist or chaplain may be called upon to lead teachers in prayer. This short service might be appropriate before a staff gathering.

LEADER   Come Holy Spirit

Come Holy Spirit, fill the hearts of your faithful and kindle in them the fire of your love. Send forth your Spirit and they shall be created.

And You shall renew the face of the earth.

O, God, who by the light of the Holy Spirit, did instruct the hearts of the faithful, grant that by the same Holy Spirit we may be truly wise and ever enjoy His consolations, Through Christ Our Lord, Amen.

READING   Mt 5:14–16
A city built on a hilltop cannot be hidden

TEACHER'S PRAYER

I want to teach my students how to live this life on earth,
to face its struggles and its strife and improve their worth.
Not just the lesson in a book or how the rivers flow,
but how to choose the proper path wherever they may go.
To understand eternal truth and know the right from wrong
and gather all the beauty of a flower and a song.

For if I help the world to grow in wisdom and grace
then I shall feel that I have won and I have filled my place.
And so I ask your guidance, God
that I may do my part for character and confidence
and happiness of heart.
Amen.

Let us pray for the coming of God's kingdom as Jesus taught us.

Our Father

Our Father, Who art in heaven
Hallowed be Thy Name;
Thy kingdom come,
Thy will be done,
on earth as it is in heaven.
Give us this day our daily bread,
and forgive us our trespasses,
as we forgive those who trespass against us;
and lead us not into temptation,
but deliver us from evil. Amen.

CONCLUDING PRAYER

God, You are the light of the world.
Look down on your children with love and mercy.
Use your light to guide us on the path you have laid out for us.
Be with us as we strive to teach, that our students may grow in wisdom and knowledge.
We ask this through Christ our Lord. Amen

A SERVICE OF HARVEST THANKSGIVING

Scripture texts and music suggestions can be found in the Appendix

Many of our students now live far from the land and may not always appreciate fully the significance or value of the harvest time. This may be an opportunity to remind them of how dependent we are on the produce of the land. It may be a good way to conclude a module of religious education that involves respect and care for the environment as it speaks of the value of God's creation.

As the service begins, an appropriately decorated worship space can be prepared with greenery and produce of the land. At the centre of the worship space there should be an empty basket, which we can call the basket of God's bounty. Each student who is participating could be given an item of produce – fruit, vegetable, flower, hay, wheat or something that represents the harvest of their area. At the appropriate point in the liturgy they can individually place their item in the basket until it overflows.

OPENING PRAYER

God of generosity and abundance we gather in your presence to express our gratitude for your harvest and for all the good things that you give us to sustain us in life. The harvest is a sign of your love for us. Help us to respond with the same generosity and love to our brothers and sisters in need. We ask this through Jesus Christ Our Lord. Amen

READING   Deuteronomy 26:1–4

When you come into the land which the Lord gives you

HARVEST THANKS

One by one students place their item of produce/symbol of harvest in the basket of God's bounty while saying aloud a harvest prayer. (These harvest prayers could be put on an index-card and distributed to the students in advance – try to have a different prayer for each student, or better still get them to compose the prayer themselves – the following are offered as suggestions)

Thank you generous God, for all you give us in the Harvest.

Help us, God, to always appreciate the gifts you give us.

May we never take our food for granted, Lord.

Teach us, loving God, to share with those in need.

Give us, O Lord, a generous and loving Spirit.

Help us to hunger for justice as we do for food.

Compassionate God, use us to bring food to those who have none.

Creator Father, give us the vision to see the beauty of nature more clearly.

Loving Jesus, teach us respect for the environment.

God the Spirit, guide the work of those who work the land for our benefit.

God of all seasons, nurture us as you nurture the seeds of life.

Guide us, O Christ, to those who hunger for love and justice.

Help us, God, to trust that you will provide for our needs in the future.

Spirit of God, give us the strength to participate in the works of the harvest.

Make all our talents. O God, part of this season's harvest.

Help us to appreciate all those who provide for us and our needs.

Give us the vision to protect the earth for those who will come after us.

Help us, God, to turn our swords into ploughshares that we may be people of peace.

Plant the seed of your word in our hearts that we may live our lives in service of you.

Bring to fruition, O Lord, all that we start in your name.

THE LORD'S PRAYER

Let us pray to our Father in heaven that he may grant us our daily bread as his so Jesus taught us to do.

Our Father, Who art in heaven
Hallowed be Thy Name;
Thy kingdom come,
Thy will be done,
on earth as it is in heaven.
Give us this day our daily bread,
and forgive us our trespasses,
as we forgive those who trespass against us;
and lead us not into temptation,
but deliver us from evil. Amen.

CONCLUDING PRAYER

Gracious God, in our gratitude for the harvest you give us, we remember those who hunger for food, for justice, for love. Forgive us the times we have been too pre-occupied to remember your goodness to us. We are grateful for all those who worked to provide for us. May we never fail to see God in the needs of others. We ask this through Christ our Lord. Amen

FEAST OF ALL SAINTS – HEROES OF FAITH

Scripture texts and music suggestions can be found in the Appendix

INTRODUCTION

Loving God, Today we honour the men and women of faith who courageously lived out the teachings of Christ in their lives. They now live with God in Heaven and we pray that you will give us their guidance and inspiration as we struggle with our Christian lives. We ask this in the name of Jesus the Lord. Amen

READING   Jn 11: 25–26
                 Whoever believes will never die.

Items/symbols you will need to accompany the litany
1.   Mary: a rosary
2.   St Joseph: a carpenter's tool
3.   Apostles: a bishop's/shepherd's staff
4.   Martyrs: a red rose
5.   Founders: a catechism
6.   Teachers: a catechism
7.   Holy men and women: a Bible
8.   Saints of Ireland: a St Bridget's Cross

LITANY OF THE SAINTS
(This should be copied and distributed to all participants)

LEADER   We turn to the examples of our heroes of faith. We try to learn from their lives and examples so that we may receive the same reward – the fullness of life with our loving God.

God our Father, Creator of Heaven and Earth
Have mercy on us.

Jesus Christ, Son of God, Redeemer of us all.
Have mercy on us.

Spirit of the Living God
Have mercy on us.

Most Holy Trinity, One God.
Have mercy on us.

(A Symbol of the Saints could be placed in a prominent place as they are invoked)

1. Mary said yes to God when He called on her. She trusted in God's promise and risked everything for love of Him –

   Holy Mary Mother of God *(Symbol – rosary)*
   Pray for us.

2. God put His Son into the loving and protective care of an honest and decent man –

   St Joseph, protector of the Christ-child. *(Symbol – A carpenter's tool)*
   Pray for us.

3. The mission of Jesus was continued by those he gathered around him and to whom he gave the gift of the Holy Spirit –

   Saints Peter and Paul, St John and all Holy Apostles *(Symbol – A bishop's/shepherd's staff)*
   Pray for us.

4. In the history of the Church many paid with their lives for believing in Jesus. Their faith was so strong that their love of God was stronger that their love of life itself –

   St Stephen, St Agnes, St Maximillian Kolbe and all Holy Martyrs. *(Symbol – a red rose)*
   Pray for us.

5.   In every generation people responded to the call to build up God's Kingdom. In their ministry they gathered people around them to help –

St Francis, St Dominic, St Ignatius and all Holy Founders *(Symbol – A cross)*
Pray for us.

6.   Many dedicated their lives to the service of young people. The strove to help all to mature in faith and knowledge of God –

St John Bosco, Blessed Edmund Rice and all Holy Teachers *(Symbol – A catechism)*
Pray for us.

7.   People of prayer always draw us closer to God by their acts of worship and devotion –

St Clare, St Thérèse of Lisieux and all Holy Men and Women of Prayer *(Symbol – A Bible)*
Pray for us.

8.   The faith we have received has been preserved and handed on by people to us down through the generations, often at great cost to themselves –

St Patrick, St Bridget, St Oliver and all Holy Men and Women of Ireland *(Symbol – A St Bridget's cross)*
Pray for us.

Lamb of God, You take away the sins of the World
Have mercy on us.

Lamb of God, You take away the sins of the World
Have mercy on us.

Lamb of God, You take away the sins of the World
Grant us peace.

Let us Pray

God of our Ancestors, your holy saints are present to us as we gather today. Give us the courage to follow their example. Guide us in the ways of faith that we might lead others to you through Christ our Lord. Amen.

A SERVICE OF REMEMBRANCE

Scripture texts and music suggestions can be found in the Appendix

This can be used as a memorial service for someone who has died within or close to the school community. It can be used within the context of a Eucharistic Celebration.

ENVIRONMENT

With a little research we can find some information about the deceased. We can establish a visual focus with a photo of the person who has died and some incense burning in front of the photo. Symbols of hobbies, interests, achievements, work can be gathered together. The celebrant can use this as people gather or as part of the homily. Be sure that the celebrant is informed exactly of the significance of the objects gathered – under no circumstances should he/she try to guess or assume.

WORDS OF WELCOME

Friends, we gather here in the protective shelter of God's healing love. We are free to express our grief, release our anger, face our emptiness and know that God cares. We gather to comfort one another in our shared loss. We commend N. to God's care and keeping as we try to have hope in Christ's resurrection.

PENITENTIAL RITE

You raise the dead to life in the Spirit. Lord have mercy.
Lord have mercy.

You bring healing and comfort to the broken-hearted. Christ have mercy.
Christ have mercy.

You give hope and confidence to all who despair. Lord have mercy.
Lord have mercy.

OPENING PRAYER

Compassionate and loving God, you love us with an everlasting love and can turn the shadow of death into the light and hope of a new day. We gather to commend N. into your gracious hands. We turn to you with broken but believing hearts. We trust in your great promises to us through Jesus, who died that we might live, and who rose from the dead that we might never die, but live always in the joy and peace of your kingdom forever and ever. Amen.

FIRST READING   Lamentations 3:17–24
The Word of the Lord

RESPONSORIAL PSALM

Psalm 23
Response: The Lord is my shepherd, there is nothing I shall want.

GOSPEL   John 14:1–7

PRAYERS OF INTERCESSION

CELEBRANT   Source of all mercies and giver of all comfort, deal graciously with all who mourn so that casting their cares on you they may know the consolation of your love.

1.   We pray for N. who has died. Bring him/her to that place where there is eternal life and peace in God's presence. Lord hear us.

2.   Bless all who mourn for N. and are heart-broken by his passing. Use their memories as instruments of God's healing grace. Lord hear us.

3.   Watch over all the members of this school community, which has been greatly saddened by the death of N. Give us the hope that comes from our Christian faith. Lord hear us.

4.   Grant us the grace to help and comfort those who find themselves desolate and lead us with them in the paths of hope. Lord hear us.

5.   Give us the grace to care for one another, to forgive anything that needs forgiving, to share all that needs sharing and to live in the peace of God. Lord hear us.

CELEBRANT   Lord Jesus, help us remember that there is a world beyond our sight, but not beyond our love. It is a world where lost things are found and broken things are mended, a world where all we have willed of good exists forever and ever. Amen.

REFLECTION

Do not stand at my grave and weep
I am not there, I do not sleep,
I am a thousand winds that blow.
I am the diamond glints on snow,
I am the sunlight on the ripened grain
I am the gentle autumn's rain.

When you awaken in the morning hush
I am the swift uplifting rush
of quiet birds in circled flight.
I am the soft stars that shine at night.
Do not stand at my grave and cry
I am not here, I do not die.

or

I'm Free
Don't grieve for me, for now I'm free
I'm following the path God laid for me.
I took his hand when I heard him call;
I turned my back and left it all.
I could not stay another day
to laugh, to love, to work or play.

Tasks left undone must stay that way;
I found my place at the close of day.
If my parting has left a void,
then fill it with remembered joy.
A friendship shared, a laugh, a kiss
Ah yes, these things I too will miss
Be not burdened with times of sorrow
I wish you the sunshine of tomorrow
My life's been full, I savoured much
Good friends, good times, a loved one's touch
Perhaps my time seems all too brief,
Don't lengthen it now with undue grief.
Lift up your heart and share with me.
God wanted me now, he set me free.

Linda Jo Jackson

CONCLUDING PRAYER

O God, whose days are without end, and whose mercies cannot be numbered, make us deeply sensitive to the shortness and uncertainty of human life. Lighten the darkness that comes from the death of N. Touch all our hearts with your love that the springs of compassion may flow and give us hope in new life through Christ our Lord. Amen.

ADVENT SERVICE OF RECONCILIATION

Scripture texts and music suggestions can be found in the Appendix

INTRODUCTION

We gather here in this season of Advent, a time to be renewed as we prepare to celebrate the birth of Jesus. Today we examine our lives honestly and ask for a true conversion of heart that we may walk again in newness of life.

OPENING PRAYER

Almighty and merciful God, you have brought us together to receive your forgiveness in our time of need. Open our eyes to see the harm we have done and give us a new heart to love you and each other. We ask this through Christ our Lord. Amen.

GOSPEL   John 3:14–21
        The Gospel of the Lord

EXAMINATION OF CONSCIENCE

We will try to look at our lives and find the things that we can change that will help make us better people in our relationships with God and those around us.

GOD   Have I always had time for God in my life? Do I try to say some prayers regularly? Are there other things in my life that take priority?

OTHERS   Do I try to be fair and honest in my dealings with others? Have I ever said or done anything that hurt someone else? Have I ever been unfair to someone else? Do I do all the things that are expected of me at home and school? Am I honest with my parents and those in authority over me? Do I always help out when it's needed? Have I always spoken well of others and respected their good name? Do I always respect property that is not my own?

SELF   Do respect the life that God has given me or are there times when I do things that are not good for me? Am I careful to respect my body and care for it, not polluting it by over-indulgence in food, drink or drugs?

Invitation to students to come to receive the sacrament of reconciliation should be warm and open.

INDIVIDUAL CONFESSION

Bless me Father for I have sinned.
I want to say sorry to God for the time I have neglected to think of Him.
I want to ask forgiveness for the times I have said or done anything that might have hurt somebody else.
I am sorry for anything that has shown disrespect for myself or my own personal growth.

Here student can mention something in particular

For these and all my sins, I am truly sorry and ask God's forgiveness.

OUR FATHER

EXCHANGE OF A SIGN OF PEACE

REFLECTION

Unforgiveness

Nothing is as painful,
As unforgiveness to the soul;
A heart that's torn asunder,
With forgiveness becomes whole.
A single kind word spoken
Means more than countless words;
The three words, 'I forgive you,'
Are all that need to be heard.
To a soul that has been wounded,
Like a healing, cooling balm;
Forgiveness soothes and comforts,
Till at last the soul is calm.
For the soul that seeks forgiveness,
When forgiveness can't be found;
It struggles vainly everyday,
To hear that simple sound.
The power in those three kind words,
Can heal a heart that's broken;
But that heart cannot begin to heal,
As long as words remain unspoken.
Compassion in its purest sense,
Reside in those three words;
The three words, 'I forgive you,'
Are all that need to be heard.

Allison Chambers Coxsey

CONCLUDING PRAYER

Father of life, the birth of your son brought new life and hope to the world. As we prepare to celebrate that great event we thank you for the sense of new life and hope that comes from being reconciled to you. Bless us as we try to grow in your love. We ask this through Christ our Lord. Amen.

VOICES OF CHRISTMAS

Music suggestions can be found in the Appendix

This could be used during Advent. Each of the speakers could place a symbol that represents them in a central place.

Items/symbols that you may need:

1. *Shepherd: a shepherd's staff*
2. *Joseph: a carpenter's tool*
3. *Innkeeper: a bunch of keys*
4. *Mary: swaddling clothes*
5. *Wise man: gift*
6. *Herod: toy sword*

SHEPHERD   We were watching our flock up in the hills. The night was mild and the sky was bright with stars. I remember we were talking about the census and the crowd of strangers it had brought to town. Suddenly there was a blaze of light – like nothing we had ever seen before. Then we saw the angel standing in the midst of it! The angel spoke in a voice of gentleness and power: 'Don't be afraid! I am here with good news for you, which will bring great joy to all the people. This very day in David's town your Saviour was born – Christ the Lord!' There was more – things I didn't understand – about swaddling clothes and a baby in a manger. And there was music. Not the thin sound of a shepherd's flute, but the glorious thunder of a heavenly choir as a great army of heaven's angels sang praises to God: 'Glory to God in the highest heaven, and peace on earth to those with whom God is pleased!' As suddenly as the first angel had appeared the great choir was gone and we were alone with the sheep and the twinkling stars. We looked at one another in wonder. Had it all been a dream? Or was this truly the night of our salvation? 'Let's go to Bethlehem' I said at last.

JOSEPH

I don't think I'll ever understand what has happened to me during these past months. I was looking forward to marriage with Mary, my betrothed. And then she told me she was pregnant! My world came tumbling around my ears for the shame of it and the bitter disappointment. She had some crazy story about the Holy Spirit! Did she think I was born yesterday? Better she had told the truth. But I didn't want to disgrace her publicly. While I was thinking, wondering what to do, an angel came to me in a dream and assured me that Mary spoke the truth! The son she would bear would be named Jesus and he would save his people from their sins. So we were married and awaited the birth with eagerness. The time was close when the census was called. Bethlehem was the place of my ancestors, and there we must go. I prayed that the baby would wait until we reached the town and then, until we found a place. 'No room' was the answer wherever we went – no room – and time running out. And then a stable a humble place, but warm and dry.

INNKEEPER

You can't blame me – though many have. Times were hard and the census seemed heaven-sent: a chance to recoup losses and lay something by for the future. Sure I felt sorry for them – an anxious Galilean and his bride heavily pregnant. But what could I do? The inn was full; guests who had paid were not about to give up their rooms to the likes of them. I did what I could. There was the stable – take it or leave it. They took it, grateful even for a patch of straw. How was I to know that history would be made in that unlikely outhouse?

MARY

It was strange how I had no doubts after the angel's visit. God had chosen me to bear his son. Poor Joseph! Angry at first, then puzzled, then sharing my wonder if not my confidence. I remember little of the journey to Bethlehem. Just as well — what I do remember is painful with the jolting of each slow step on the dusty road. I remember Joseph's desperation as he went from door to door and always the same answer: 'No room! Don't you know there's a census?' The warmth of the stable welcomed us, offered rest at last. Thus Jesus was born and I looked in wonder at God's own son. A shadow fell across the doorway and shepherds came to gaze in awe and tell their story of angel songs. Having grown used to angels I did not doubt them. They left, singing praise to God for all they had heard and seen.

WISE-MAN

In the east we believe that the stars point to the great events of history. I will never forget the first night that I saw what must have been the brightest star I have ever seen. Surely it must indicate an event of great importance. This star almost touched the earth. I felt it calling; I was being compelled to follow its direction. On my journey I met with two others who had seen and followed the same star. Finally after many months we reached the land of Israel. We sought information from a local leader, a man by the name of Herod. He seemed anxious that we should share all our information with him and he sent us on to Bethlehem. The star seemed to hover over a stable and as we came to it we saw a couple and their newborn son. They seemed so much at peace. This was the birth that would change the course of history. We left them gifts of gold, frankincense, and myrrh. We were about to return to tell Herod when we were visited by an angel warning us to make another way home for the safety of the child.

HEROD

I've just had the strangest visit. Three astrologers from the east claimed to have followed a star to this country. They believed that it signalled an event that would change history. I called the religious leaders and asked them what it could mean. They thought it might have something to do with the Jewish Messiah.

The Jews believe that God will raise up a leader for his people and he is to save them. They are going on to Bethlehem where the Messiah is supposed to be born. As far as I'm concerned I'm top dog around here and no messiah is going to take my throne. I've pretended to the astrologers that I am interested in honouring the Messiah so I have asked them to come back and tell me where he is. He won't last long while I have a say.

INTER~FAITH SERVICE

Music suggestions can be found in the Appendix

This service could be used in a number of contexts. An understanding of the five major world religions is often studied as part of the catechetical programme. This service could be used after having studied them in class. Children from many cultures and faiths are now forming an increasing part of our school communities. This service, or parts of it, could be used when a liturgy is celebrated integrating children from other religious traditions. There is a prayer for peace from each tradition included in the text. Each of the religions could be represented by an appropriate symbol.

* * * * *

HINDUISM

Hinduism, the world's oldest religion, has no beginning – it precedes recorded history. It is a mystical religion, leading the follower to personally experience the Truth within. While acknowledging many Gods, all Hindus believe in a one Supreme God who creates and sustains the universe. There are about 700 million Hindus in the world today.

Karma is another important belief by which each individual creates his/her own destiny by his/her thoughts, words and deeds. Reincarnation of the soul is key to Hindu belief.

All life is sacred, to be loved and revered, and therefore Hindus practise *ahimsa*, 'non-injury.'

HINDU PRAYER FOR PEACE

Lead us from the unreal to the Real.
Lead us from darkness to light.

Lead us from death to immortality.

Peace, Peace, Peace unto all.

May there be peace in celestial regions.

May there be peace on Earth.

May the waters be appeasing.

May herbs be wholesome,

and may trees and plants bring peace to all.

May all beneficent beings bring peace to us.

May thy Law propagate peace

all through the world.

May all things be a source of peace to us.

And may thy peace itself, bestow peace on all

and may that peace come to me also.

* * * * *

BUDDHISM

Buddhism is the fourth largest religion in the world. It was founded in Northern India by the Buddha, Siddhartha Gautama. He was born about 563 BC in modern-day Nepal. At the age of twenty-nine, he left his wife, children and political involvements in order to seek truth. It was an accepted practice at the time for some men to leave their family and lead the life of an ascetic. He attained enlightenment and assumed the title 'Buddha' ('one who has awakened').

He promoted The Middle Way, as a path toward the state of Nirvana. He had many disciples and accumulated a large public following by the time of his death. Two and a half centuries later, a council of Buddhist monks collected his teachings and the oral traditions of the faith into written form, called the Tripitaka.

One fundamental belief involves reincarnation: the concept that one must go through many cycles of birth, living, and death. After many such cycles, if a person releases their attachment to desire and the self, they can attain Nirvana – a state of liberation and freedom from suffering.

May all beings everywhere plagued

with sufferings of body and mind

quickly be freed from their illnesses.

May those frightened cease to be afraid,

and may those bound be free.

May the powerless find power,

and may people think of befriending one another.

May those who find themselves in trackless, fearful wilderness –

the children, the aged, the unprotected –

be guarded by beneficial celestials,

and may they swiftly attain Buddhahood.

* * * * *

JUDAISM

Around 2000 BC, the God of the ancient Israelites established a divine agreement or covenant with Abraham, making him the father of many nations. Moses led his people out of captivity in Egypt, and received the Law from God. After decades of wandering through wilderness, Joshua led the tribes into the promised land.

The original tribal organization was converted into a kingdom by Samuel; its first king was Saul. The second king, David, established Jerusalem as the religious and political center. The third king, Solomon built the first temple there.

There are currently about 18 million Jews throughout the world. They are mainly concentrated in North America (about 7 million) and Israel (about 4.5 million).

Jewish people observe the Sabbath as a day of rest which commences at sundown on Friday evening. Passover is one of the most important festivals in the Jewish calendar when we recall our deliverance from slavery in Egypt.

Come let us go up to the mountain of the Lord, that we may walk the paths of the Most High. And we shall beat our swords into ploughshares and our spears into pruning hooks. Nation shall not lift up sword against nation — neither shall they learn war any more. And none shall be afraid, for the mouth of the Lord of Hosts has spoken.

Grant us peace. Your most precious gift, O Eternal Source of peace, and give us the will to proclaim its message to all the peoples of the earth. Bless our country, that it may always be a stronghold of peace, and its advocate among the nations. May contentment reign within its borders, health and happiness within its homes. Strengthen the bonds of friendship among the inhabitants of all lands. And may the love of Your name hallow every home and every heart. Blessed is the Eternal God, the source of Peace.

* * * * *

CHRISTIANITY

To be a Christian is to follow teachings of and about Jesus of Nazareth commonly referred to as Jesus Christ. (Christ is Greek for 'the Messiah' or the 'anointed one.') Jesus was a Jewish itinerant preacher who was was executed by the Roman occupying authorities in Palestine. Most Christians regard him as the son of God. They further believe that he is God, the second person in the Trinity. Most Christians believe that Jesus co-existed with God before the creation of the world, was born of a virgin, was resurrected three days after his death, and later ascended to Heaven.

The Roman Empire recognised Christianity as a valid religion in 313 AD. The Protestant Reformation in the sixteenth century led to a split within the Western Church. The Protestant movement further fragmented into what is now thousands of individual denominations and groups of denominations. At present almost 33 per cent of the world's population profess a belief in Jesus of Nazareth.

Lord, make me an instrument of your peace.
Where there is hatred, let me sow love,
Where there is injury, pardon,
Where there is doubt, faith,
Where there is despair, hope,
Where there is darkness, light,
where there is sadness, joy.

O Divine Master,
grant that I may not so much seek
To be consoled as to console,
To be understood as to understand,
To be loved as to love.
For it is in giving that we receive,
It is in pardoning that we are pardoned,
It is in dying that we are born to eternal life.

* * * * *

ISLAM

Islam is an Arabic word which means to surrender oneself totally and completely to the will of Allah. Those who follow the Islamic faith are called Muslims. There are about 1.2 billion followers of Islam throughout the world. The primary Muslim belief is that, 'There is no God but Allah and Muhammad is His prophet'. This is the cornerstone of our belief. It is called the *Shahada* – the testimony of faith.

The good Muslim tries to lead a life of prayer. It is also important for them to contribute to the support of the poor and to fast during the month of Ramadan. They also try to make a pilgrimage to the Holy city of Mecca where the prophet Muhammad came from. The sacred text is called the Qu'ran. This is the revealed word of God to the prophet Muhammad. The Muslim also has great respect for the Sunnah, which is all that the prophet Muhammad said or did or approved of.

Muslims perform five prayers a day. Each prayer does not take more than a few minutes to perform. Prayer in Islam is a direct link between the worshipper and God.

MUSLIM PRAYER FOR PEACE

In the name of Allah,
the beneficent, the merciful.
Praise be to the Lord of the
Universe who has created us and
made us into tribes and nations
That we may know each other, not that
we may despise each other.
If the enemy incline towards peace, do
thou also incline towards peace, and
trust God, for the Lord is the one that
heareth and knoweth all things.
And the servants of God,
Most gracious are those who walk on
the Earth in humility, and when we
address them, we say 'PEACE'.

CONCLUDING PRAYER

When we gather in peace to pray and worship we touch the divine. May this divine spirit touch all our lives to make us people of peace so that the world may be a better place for all to live. May this same divine spirit enlighten the minds of all who govern in our world to promote peace and harmony among peoples of every race, language and way of life.

PRAYER FOR PEACE

Scripture texts and music suggestions can be found in the Appendix

INTRODUCTION

Many parts of our world are troubled and long for peace. War and violence are an everyday reality for many of God's children. Poverty and despair are all that some people on our planet can realistically expect. Homes and families are destroyed in lands where evil thrives. We gather to pray for and remember all who are troubled and live in fear. We think too of all who lead and guide our world. We remember those who have given their lives as victims of war or in the service of justice and peace.

Items/Symbols you will need:
1. The Paschal Candle
2. A map of the world
3. A weapon (e.g. a toy gun/sword)
4. A child's toy (something that represents simplicity, innocence, e.g. a teddy bear)
5. A bundle of belongings (representing refugees)
6. A handkerchief (representing those who weep)

OPENING PRAYER

God of life and peace
You draw life and death together in yourself.
Watch over your creation
Listen to your children who cry to you
Especially those who are bloodied by battle and weary of war.
Be with us as we gather, guide us as we pray and strengthen us in our resolve to work
For peace and justice.
We ask this through Christ our Lord. Amen.

LIGHTING OF THE PASCHAL CANDLE

After his resurrection, Jesus appeared to his disciples. Each time his greeting was the same, 'Peace be with you.' As we light the paschal candle, which is the symbol of Christ's resurrection, we pray that this light of peace may shine in the parts of the world darkened by war, violence and hatred.

FIRST READING Isaiah 2:4
The Word of the Lord

RESPONSORIAL PSALM

Psalm 95:1–2; 3–5
Response: The Lord judges the people with fairness

GOSPEL

John 14:27–29
The Gospel of the Lord

PROCESSION FOR PEACE

1.   We bring to the light of Christ a map of the world.

We ask Christ to shed the light of his love and peace in the places darkened by war and violence. Cast the light of your wisdom on the men and women who struggle to lead justly and fairly. Give the light of courage to those who strive for peace and justice.

2.   We bring to the light of Christ a weapon.

May those who inflict violence to be drawn by the prospect of peace. Sustain and strengthen our peacekeepers and give the light of eternal light to all who have died as victims of war.

3.   We bring to the light of Christ a child's toy.

We pray in solidarity with the innocent children whose lives are impoverished because of war. Give your fatherly care to those who have been orphaned and send your protection to those who continue to live in fear.

4.   We bring to the light of Christ a bundle of belongings.

We pray for refugees of war, uprooted and forced to find a new home or homeland. Give to all of them the light of guidance. Instill in the hearts of all a sense of welcome and openess.

5.   We bring to the light of Christ a handkerchief.

We pray for all in the world who weep because of war. Give the light of comfort to all who have suffered loss. Do not let the tears of your brothers and sisters go unheard.

REFLECTION

TEACH US TO LIVE

God of love – Forgive! Forgive!
Teach us how to truly live
Ask us not our race or creed,
Just take us in our hour of need,
And let us know you love us too,
And that we are all a part of you,
And someday may man realise,
That all the Earth; the seas and skies
Belong to god who made us all,
The rich, the poor, the great, the small.
And in the Father's holy sight
No man is yellow, black or white

And peace on earth cannot be found
Until we meet on common ground
And every man becomes a brother
Who worships God and loves each other.

Helen Steiner Rice
from *Prayerfully, Poems of Devotion*

CLOSING PRAYER

God of peace, justice and infinite mercy,
We ask you to enfold our planet in peace and truth.
Enlighten the minds of all who make decisions.
Melt the hearts of those who inflict cruelty on your children
and strengthen the resolve of all who pray for peace.
We ask this through Christ our Lord. Amen.

BLESSING

May the Lord bless us and all with whom we share the Earth, the Father, the Son
and the Holy Spirit. Amen.

OUR FATHER

Music suggestions can be found in the Appendix

The Our Father is probably one of the most common prayers recited throughout the world. Sometimes we say it without ever reflecting on what it means. This liturgy provides students with the opportunity to reflect not only on the Our Father, but on the role of prayer in their lives.

INTRODUCTION

The Our Father is called the Lord's Prayer because the Lord Jesus himself gave it to his apostles. It is the model and pattern of what our prayer should be like. It contains all that we should ask God for to help us in our lives.

READER 1   **Our Father, Who art in Heaven**

God in Heaven we call you Father because you have created us. Since you are our Father we are all brothers and sisters of each other. This means we should treat each other with love and respect. You sent Jesus into the world to be our brother and our friend. He is the example of what it means to be a true child of the Father in Heaven. Help us, God, to always have that childlike trust in you so that we may grow in your love and live with you one day in heaven.

READER 2   **Hallowed be thy name**

Loving God, you made us to know love and serve you in this life so that we could be happy with you forever in the next life. We glorify your name and show respect for you because of all you have done for us. We respect your name and regard it as holy. May the respect we show to your name lead others to create a place for you in their lives.

READER 3   **Thy Kingdom come**

Father, we pray that your name may be known and loved throughout the world. You rule over a kingdom where truth and justice are important. We will try to promote these same values of your kingdom here on earth. We pray that your kingdom may grow throughout the world that people may experience your love everywhere on the earth.

READER 4   **Thy will be done on earth, as it is in Heaven**

Loving God, The angels and saints in heaven are especially close to you in love. They are there because they loved you greatly while they were on this earth. We hope and pray for the grace to do your will in our lives; to obey your commandments and to follow the example of your Son Jesus Christ. Your love for us has no limits. Help us to see what you wish for us even in the times of life that are difficult. Help us always to make the right choices that lead to You.

READER 5   **Give us this day our daily bread**

Almighty God, Jesus taught us to turn in prayer to you for anything we need. He said, 'Ask and you shall receive, seek and you shall find.' You know all that we need to help us live our lives. Teach us to be generous with the world's resources so that we can share with those who struggle for the necessities of life.

READER 6   **Forgive us our trespasses**

Forgiving God, when we commit sin we turn away from your love. Give us the grace to see the forgiveness you offer to those who are truly sorry for the things they have done wrong. Help us to change our lives, give us a spirit of repentance that we may draw closer to you.

READER 7   **As we forgive those who trespass against us**

God of Justice, there are people in all our lives who have hurt us or let us down. We have all experienced anger and resentment towards others. Help us to overcome these feelings so that we may be people of love and forgiveness like our Father in heaven.

READER 8   **And lead us not into temptation**

God of power and might, when your son Jesus was tempted in the desert you sent your angels to protect him. Help us to avoid people, places and things that might lead us into sin. Let no-one or nothing ever come between us and the love of God.

READER 9   **But deliver us from evil.**

Caring God, keep us safe from the things that are hurtful or harmful. Protect us from illness, from accidents and from every other evil. Keep us in your watchful loving care that we may grow in love of you and in respect for all you have created.

CONCLUDING PRAYER

Jesus Christ has given us the Our Father as the model of all prayer. Keep us faithful to your teaching so that we may live in our lives the faith that we speak with our lips. We ask this with the help of God's Holy Spirit who lives and reigns forever and ever. Amen.

LENTEN RECONCILIATION SERVICE

Scripture texts and music suggestions can be found in the Appendix

ENVIRONMENT

Stations for individual confession should be set up around the church/prayer area. Each station may be designated by two chairs, and/or a small table covered in purple cloth. In the sanctuary area, light one candle for each confessor. At the time of individual confession, the confessors come forward, take a candle and go to their station, placing it on the table there. When each confessor has completed his ministry he can return the candle to its original position. Since we will be using the Ten Commandment as the basis for our examination of conscience we could use a representation of the two tablets of stone received by Moses as a visual focus.

INTRODUCTION

A pure heart create for us, O Lord, and put a steadfast spirit within us. We come together in this season of Lent to seek God's forgiveness. By the sacrament of reconciliation God will heal our wounds and take away all that divides us. This he does through the love of Jesus Christ in the power of the Holy Spirit.

OPENING PRAYER

We pray to you, O Lord, for the grace of your forgiveness. You are our refuge in times of distress. Let your spirit of repentance come down on us and release us from the burden of our past. Help us to follow your path, for you live and reign forever and ever. Amen.

READING	Joel 2:12–14a
	The Word of the Lord

EXAMINATION OF CONSCIENCE

This examination is based on the Ten Commandments and can be led by three readers; Reader 1 to announce the commandment, Reader 2 to explain the teaching and Reader 3 to propose the examination.

READER 1	I am the Lord your God. You shall not have strange gods before me.
READER 2	The first commandment teaches us to put God first in our lives.
READER 3	Do I regard God as important in my life or am I more concerned with other things like money, position or power?

READER 1	You shall not take the name of the Lord your God in vain.
READER 2	The second commandment teaches to respect the name of God and his Son Jesus and to respect the power of our words.
READER 3	Do I use the holy name in an irreverent or careless way? Do I use bad language too much? Do I speak to others in a disrespectful way?
READER 1	Remember the keep holy the sabbath day.
READER 2	The third commandment teaches us to take time to worship God regularly.
READER 3	Do I make a decent effort to spend time in prayer and acknowledge my need of God?

READER 1	Honour your father and your mother.
READER 2	The fourth commandment teaches us to appreciate our parents.
READER 3	Do I show respect for my parents and all who have a duty of care towards me?
READER 1	You shall not kill.
READER 2	The fifth commandment teaches us to appreciate life.
READER 3	Do I value all people and avoid things that harm the life I have been given?
READER 1	You shall not commit adultery.
READER 2	The sixth commandment teaches us to keep our promise and respect our sexuality.
READER 3	Do I value and respect my sexuality and try to develop healthy relationships?
READER 1	You shall not steal.
READER 2	The seventh commandment teaches us to respect private property and the rights of others.
READER 3	Do I consider the needs and rights of others when I use anything? Do I respect public property and do I share generously?
READER 1	You shall not bear false witness against your neighbour.
READER 2	The eighth commandment teaches us to always speak the truth.
READER 3	Am I truthful person? Is gossip a part of my life?
READER 1	You shall not covet your neighbour's spouse.

READER 2	The ninth commandment teaches us to avoid inappropriate relationships.
READER 3	Do I respect people's value and remember that all are created in the image and likeness of God.
READER 1	You shall not covet your neighbour's goods.
READER 2	The tenth commandment teaches us to find happiness where we are.
READER 3	Do I let envy or greed take over my life? Do I remember that is is who I am, not what I own, that is really important.

INDIVIDUAL CONFESSION

OUR FATHER

EXCHANGE OF PEACE

CONCLUDING PRAYER

Father in heaven, you bring your family together in love. Let your Spirit guide us in your commandments. Let your spirit wake up our hearts to proclaim your love. Let your spirit fill us with new life. We ask this through Christ our Lord. Amen.

THE WAY OF THE CROSS

Music suggestions can be found in the Appendix

Each year on Good Friday the Pope leads the stations of the cross at the Roman Colosseum. In this way he remembers and unites all the suffering of Christ with the suffering of the world today. In 1991, Pope John Paul II changed the format from the traditional fourteen stations that are familiar to us. In the new way of the cross there are fifteen stations, all of which are based on incidents recorded in the Gospels. Stations of the cross should, if possible, involve some sense of movement, indicating that we make the journey with Christ and all who suffer. Since most of our churches contain the images of the traditional stations, some visual symbols of the new stations might be useful in their place. These symbols can be real or they can be artistic representations. It might be possible to use a PowerPoint presentation or an overhead projector depending on your resources. Talk to some of the IT people in your school – they often enjoy a challenge like this. The visual symbols you will need are listed at the beginning of each station.

OPENING PRAYER

Lord Jesus Christ,

Be with us now as we prepare to accompany you on the journey to Calvary. Your love for us was so great that you willingly underwent the pain and suffering of the cross to save us. As we travel with you we remember all those who suffer or are in any kind of need in our world today. Bless us with your love, strengthen us with your courage and unite us with your victory over sin, suffering and death for you are Lord forever and ever.

ALL   Amen.

FIRST STATION

(Visual symbol: *chalice/cup*)

The Agony of Jesus in the Garden of Olives

LEADER	We adore you, O Christ and we praise you.
ALL	Because by your holy cross you have saved the world.
FIRST READER	After the Last Supper, Jesus went into the Garden of Olives to pray. He told the disciples with him that his soul was sorrowful to the point of death. When he prayed his fear was great. He asked God to let the cup of suffering pass him by if it were possible. He found courage in his prayer to hand over his fear to God.
SECOND READER	Lord Jesus, there are many times in life when we are afraid. We can be afraid of the future, of all that lies ahead. We can be afraid to do the right thing. Help us to hand over our fears to God. Give us the courage to face the future with confidence, knowing that God is with us every step of the way.

SECOND STATION

(Visual symbol: *thirty silver coins*)

The Betrayal and Arrest of Jesus

LEADER	We adore you, O Christ and we praise you.
ALL	Because by your holy cross you have saved the world.
FIRST READER	When Jesus had finished praying Judas came into the garden with a crowd carrying swords and clubs. Judas went up to Jesus and kissed him, saying 'Rabbi'. At this, the crowd of soldiers knew who he was and arrested him.
SECOND READER	Lord Jesus, you knew what it was like to be betrayed by a fried, someone whom you loved and trusted. Help us in the times when

we are hurt or let down. Be with us when our hearts are broken and give us the grace to by loyal and steadfast in our friendships.

THIRD STATION

(Visual symbol: *judge's gavel*)

The Sanhedrin Condemns Jesus

LEADER	We adore you, O Christ and we praise you.
ALL	Because by your holy cross you have saved the world.
FIRST READER	After he had been arrested, Jesus was brought before the chief priests and Sanhedrin, who were the religious leaders at the time. They had become jealous of Jesus' popularity among the ordinary people and wished to condemn him. They brought people who made false accusations and told lies and in this way condemned him.
SECOND READER	Lord Jesus, you were the victim of envy and jealousy. People spoke about you in an untruthful and uncharitable way and you paid the price with your life. Be with us when people say unkind or nasty things about us. Give us the courage to stand up for the truth regardless of the cost to ourselves or our pride, even if it means risking unpopularity.

FOURTH STATION

(Visual symbol: *blindfold*)

Peter Denies Jesus

LEADER	We adore you, O Christ and we praise you.
ALL	Because by your holy cross you have saved the world.
FIRST READER	Peter was one of Jesus' closest friends. After Jesus had been taken to the temple, Peter followed. While he was there, three different

people asked if he knew Jesus. Three times he denied having anything to do with Jesus or even knowing him. When the cock crowed twice to indicate the dawn, Peter realised what he had done and cried bitterly in his great sorrow.

SECOND READER   Lord Jesus, you could see that Peter was willing but weak. He loved you greatly, but fear of the consequences prevented him from supporting you openly. Guide us Lord, when our own weakness lets Jesus down. Help us to be proud of our faith in you and give us the strength to profess it before other people.

FIFTH STATION

(Visual symbol: *bowl of water and cloth*)

Pilate Condemns Jesus to the Cross

LEADER   We adore you, O Christ and we praise you.

ALL   Because by your holy cross you have saved the world.

FIRST READER   Early on Friday morning the chief priests brought Jesus before Pontius Pilate, the Roman Governor. Pilate could see that Jesus was innocent and wanted to set him free. The mob was angry and threatened Pilate demanding that Jesus be crucified. Pilate was afraid and gave in. He condemned Jesus to the cross and then washed his hands claiming to be innocent of this man's blood.

SECOND READER   Jesus, you were unjustly condemned to die like a criminal. An ugly mob turned on you and intimidated the authorities into behaving unjustly. Be with all the victims of injustice and unfairness in the world today. Guide all leaders to work for the good of those they serve.

SIXTH STATION

(Visual symbol: *whip/crown of thorns*)

Jesus is scourged and crowned with thorns.

LEADER	We adore you, O Christ and we praise you.
ALL	Because by your holy cross you have saved the world.
FIRST READER	Even before his crucifixion Jesus was subjected to a most cruel punishment. He was whipped and beaten, the skin torn from his back. Mocking him, they said, 'the King must have a crown'. And so they made one from long sharp thorns which they pushed onto his head, piercing his scalp, causing even more pain.
SECOND READER	Lord, you endured the emotional pain of betrayal, denial and condemnation. Now begins the physical pain and suffering. Watch over all those who are ill or suffer in any physical way. Watch over and protect all who care for the sick and infirm. Grant them the healing touch of your love.

SEVENTH STATION

(Visual symbol: *a purple cloak/cloth*)

Jesus is mocked by the soldiers and given his cross

LEADER	We adore you, O Christ and we praise you.
ALL	Because by your holy cross you have saved the world.
FIRST READER	The soldiers took Jesus away and mocked him. They pretended to do him honour as King. They blindfolded him and hit him demanding that he guess who had done it. They dressed him in a purple cloak like a king. Then they laid the cross on his shoulders.
SECOND READER	Lord Jesus, you deserved reverence and respect and yet you were humiliated and disgraced. Remind us that when slagging someone

off, or making fun of them, it can be hurtful and humiliating. Give us the grace to be sensitive to the feelings of other people.

EIGHTH STATION

(Visual symbol: *handprint=helping hand*)

Simon of Cyrene helps Jesus to carry his cross

LEADER	We adore you, O Christ and we praise you.
ALL	Because by your holy cross you have saved the world.
FIRST READER	Jesus was forced to carry his cross to the place of execution. It was heavy and he was already very weak. The soldiers could see this and pulled a man from the crowd and forced him to help. His name was Simon and he came from a place called Cyrene.
SECOND READER	Jesus, in your hour of greatest need you were helped by a stranger. He did not know you but was compelled to help. Be with us when we are challenged to help others, even people we may not know. Create in all people a sense of Christian charity and an awareness of the needs of others.

NINTH STATION

(Visual symbol: *a handkerchief*)

Jesus meets the women of Jerusalem

LEADER	We adore you, O Christ and we praise you.
ALL	Because by your holy cross you have saved the world.
FIRST READER	As Jesus made his way to the place of execution he encountered some women from Jerusalem. They were upset at his suffering and cried for his pain. He said to them, 'Women of Jerusalem, do not weep for me, but for yourselves and your children'.

SECOND READER   Lord Jesus, in your great trouble you met with others who could feel the depth of your pain and have compassion. Grant us the patience to listen to those who are troubled and the insight to feel the pain of another. Give true friends to all people in need.

TENTH STATION

(Visual symbol: *hammer and nails*)

Jesus is crucified

LEADER   We adore you, O Christ and we praise you.

ALL   Because by your holy cross you have saved the world.

FIRST READER   Finally Jesus arrives at Golgotha, the place of the skull. The soldiers stripped him of his clothes and nailed him to the cross. He hung upon the cross for three hours. It was the greatest act of love and self-sacrifice.

SECOND READER   Lord Jesus, you sacrificed yourself completely and totally in an act of love. Help us to learn from your example. Make us generous that we may give and not count the cost. Keep us mindful of the sacrifices that others make for us.

ELEVENTH STATION

(Visual symbol: *gateway/door*)

Jesus promises paradise to the repentant thief

LEADER   We adore you, O Christ and we praise you.

ALL   Because by your holy cross you have saved the world.

FIRST READER   Jesus was crucified between two thieves. One of them mocked him and jeered at him. The other defended Jesus and asked for his forgiveness. Jesus said to him, 'Today, you will be with me in paradise'.

SECOND READER
Lord Jesus, you gave forgiveness and promised paradise to the thief who asked you. Give us the insight to see that you will forgive us even when we are unable and unwilling to forgive ourselves. Remind us that it is never too late to turn to you and ask for your forgiveness.

TWELFTH STATION

(Visual symbol: *rosary/statue of Our Lady*)

Jesus speaks to his mother and to his disciple

LEADER
We adore you, O Christ and we praise you.

ALL
Because by your holy cross you have saved the world.

FIRST READER
When Jesus was hanging on the cross his mother Mary and his good friend John were among those standing there. Seeing them Jesus said to his mother, 'Woman, here is your son'. Then he said to John, 'Here is your mother'. From that moment John made a place for Mary in his home.

SECOND READER
Jesus, your mother Mary was close to you at all the significant moments of your life. From the cross you made her our mother too. Give us her care and protection at those times we need it most.

THIRTEENTH STATION

(Visual symbol: *large cross/crucifix*)

Jesus dies on the cross

LEADER
We adore you, O Christ and we praise you.

ALL
Because by your holy cross you have saved the world.

FIRST READER
Jesus had hung on the cross for three hours. He was pained and weakened, his body could endure no more. Jesus gave a loud cry and breathed his last.

SECOND READER   Lord Jesus, by dying on the cross you have shown us that even in moments of greatest despair there can be hope. You died forgiving and loving just as you had lived. Give hope to all who die. Help us to live in the hope of the new life that you offer.

FOURTEENTH STATION

(Visual symbol: *linen burial cloths*)

The burial of Jesus

LEADER   We adore you, O Christ and we praise you.

ALL   Because by your holy cross you have saved the world.

FIRST READER   After Jesus died, his body was taken down from the cross and placed in the arms of his heart-broken mother. Joseph from Arimathea, who had been a secret follower of Jesus, took the body of Jesus. They wrapped it in a linen cloth and placed it in a tomb and rolled a great stone across the entrance.

SECOND READER   Jesus, when you died your family and friends were heart-broken. All their hopes and dreams were shattered. Help all who mourn the loss of someone they love. Comfort all those who are lonely and broken-hearted. Give all of us hope that there is life beyond the grave.

FIFTEENTH STATION

(Visual symbol: *empty tomb/open tabernacle*)

Jesus rises from the dead

LEADER   We adore you, O Christ and we praise you.

ALL   Because by your holy cross you have saved the world.

FIRST READER   After the Sabbath was over some of the followers of Jesus went to the tomb. When they got there they found that the stone had been rolled away from the entrance to the tomb and the tomb was empty. An angel appeared to them and said, 'He is not here, he is risen'.

SECOND READER   Lord Jesus, your resurrection gives us great hope. Help us to see that we can always rise above our failure, triumph over our weakness and emerge victorious from our struggles in life. When we experience our own Good Friday, you risen Lord are there to carry us through to Easter Sunday.

REFLECTION

THE CROSS ROOM

The young man was at the end of his rope.
Seeing no way out, he dropped to his knees in prayer.
'Lord, I can't go on,' he said.
'I have too heavy a cross to bear.'
The Lord replied,
'My son, if you can't bear its weight,
just place your cross inside this room.
Then open another door and pick any cross you wish.'
The man was filled with relief.
'Thank you, Lord,'
he sighed and did as he was told.
As he looked around the room he saw many different crosses;
some so large the tops were not visible.
Then he spotted a tiny cross leaning against a far wall.
'I'd like that one, Lord,'
he whispered. And the Lord replied,
'My son, that's the cross you brought in.'

CONCLUDING PRAYER

Eternal and ever-loving God

We have travelled with your Son on his final journey to the cross. Help us to learn from his example of love and self-sacrifice. We ask this through Christ our Lord.

Amen.

THE VOICES OF THE PASSION

Music suggestions can be found in the Appendix

This liturgy is based on one called Voices of Easter *found on the website www.backtothebible.org. This can provide an opportunity for students to present the story of the passion, death and resurrection of Jesus in a dramatic way. This liturgy would probably be much more powerful if the students learned the parts and presented them in a more dramatic way. Why not even try costume?*

Items/symbols you may need:

1. Judas: a bag of coins
2. Pilate: a bowl of water and towel
3. Mary Magdalene: a jar of spices

INTRODUCTION

NARRATOR   Have you ever wondered what it would be like to be present at significant moments of history? What it would mean to be a first-hand witness to the great events that shaped our world? It would mean that we would have greater faith in those events. When it comes to the stories of Jesus we trust in the witness and evidence of those who were present. Sometimes if we listen to the voices of Easter we may find they echo the voices in our own lives, particularly when faced with moments of challenge or decision.

JUDAS   My name is Judas Iscariot. I was one of the closest friends of Jesus, one of the chosen twelve apostles. I had thought, like the others, that Jesus was going to overthrow the Roman power in Palestine. He must have trusted me though, because he put me in charge of the group's money. If anyone gave him money I took care of it. Sometimes the temptation was too much to resist and I used to help myself from the common fund. That way I could buy little extras for myself. We had been going around together for almost three years. We were really popular. All he had to do was say the word and we could have had a revolution. The religious leaders were worried. I thought we could bring things to a head so I offered to hand him over for thirty pieces of silver. He was in the Garden after supper, it was has favourite place to pray. I led the soldiers and the chief-priests there. I stepped forward and kissed Jesus on the cheek, greeting him in a way I had often done. He looked straight at me. He knew. He had known all along. Maybe he could forgive me, but I could not forgive myself. My name is Judas. I am the voice of betrayal – the voice of anyone who has betrayed someone they love.

Student drops bag of coins and leaves.

PETER   My name is Peter. I was known all around the sea of Galilee as the big fisherman. I had my own business, everybody knew me. Then Jesus came along and turned everything upside-down. He was different to the preachers who had come before. He was real, really close to God. Sometimes even I had difficulty believing the miracles and I was there when they happened. I'll never forget the night he was arrested, everything happened so fast. I pulled out my sword, but he made me put it back – a man of peace to the end. I followed on to where they were questioning him. Three people in the place recognised me and confronted me. I was terrified, afraid of being arrested myself, so I pretended not to even know Jesus. In fact, the third time I swore that I never even knew Jesus. Then the cock crew to signal the new day. Then I remembered what Jesus had said – he knew that I would deny him. He had said it to me, and I said 'Never'. I didn't mean to, but I was afraid. But I knew Jesus. If I get a chance, I'll tell him I'm sorry. I know he'll forgive me – he always does. My name is Peter. I am the voice of denial.

Student kneels and says 'forgive me, Jesus' and leaves.

MARY MAGDELENE Mine is the Voice of Adoration. Jesus changed my life! He loved me when no one else did. I've almost forgotten the days before! I will not speak of them: I will speak of Him. I followed Him wherever he went. I saw Him raise the dead and heal the sick. The blind saw, the lame walked, the deaf heard and the dumb spoke. Those bound by evil spirits were released by His command. But then the leaders in Jerusalem arrested Him and killed Him! I stood at His cross and watched Him die. I wept to see Him suffer. We stayed there all day – from the morning when they drove the nails through His hands and feet into the cross until it was over, and the soldier drove a spear into His side. Late in the afternoon, a strange thing happened! A member of the Sanhedrin approached the centurion in charge. (Someone said he was Joseph from Arimathea, a town just twenty miles away.) He showed the centurion a document, and the soldiers took down the body for him. We followed thisman as they carried Jesus' body to a tomb nearby. Another rich man met him, and they worked together quickly preparing the body for it was almost the Sabbath. They didn't have time to finish: there was time only for washing and wrapping. They laid Jesus' body in a new tomb. We watched, and remembered the place, for we wanted to come back and anoint the body properly.

Student leaves a jar of spices.

PONTIUS PILATE My name is Pontius Pilate. I am from a good Roman family and have served Caesar well in the Roman army. I should have a better job than this. Being Roman governor of Judea is no cake-walk. Their passionate adherence to their religion makes them almost ungovernable. They have no real respect for Roman law. They have a festival here called Passover and there is always unrest in Jerusalem. This year, the temple authorities came charging into the Praetorium with a man bound with ropes. Apparently, this man was travelling all over Palestine causing unrest. I could tell that it was the religious leaders of Jerusalem that felt threatened, but they tried to accuse him of sedition against Rome. I interviewed this man Jesus and could not find him guilty of anything. By now, a large, ugly mob had gathered outside the Praetorium. They were shouting for the prisoner to be put to death. If I didn't do something there would be a revolt. I tried to release him but the mob would have none of it. Then I had him scourged and whipped. Still they shouted for his death. I was afraid that if I didn't give in, I would have to face a greater problem. I knew he was innocent, but still I signed the order for his crucifixion. I am Pontius Pilate. I am the voice of cowardice.

Student brings jug and bowl and towel and pours the water over Pilate's hands, who dries them with the towel.

DISMAS

My name is Dismas. I am a Jew from a poor family. Ever since I was a young boy I found that stealing was the easiest way to make ends meet. I fell in with the wrong crowd. Sure, I was bound to end up on a cross under Roman law. There is no doubt but this man on the cross beside me does not belong here. I can hear him pray. He speaks comfortably with God. He's no thief, no criminal. Maybe he is the Messiah, the Son of God. I ask him to pray for me, to remember me. He promised me that I would join him in paradise. You know something, I believe him. My name is Dismas – I am the voice of faith.

Student says 'Jesus remember me' and bows his head before leaving.

CONCLUDING PRAYER

Loving God, we have listened to the voices of those who witnessed the death of your son Jesus Christ. We have heard the voices of betrayal, denial and cowardice. We have heard too, the voice of faith. Strengthen our faith in the love of your Son Jesus Christ who is Lord forever and ever. Amen.

PENTECOST

A CELEBRATION OF GOD'S SPIRIT IN ALL CREATION

Scripture texts and music suggestions can be found in the Appendix

In this liturgy, we celebrate the gift of God's spirit as it is present in all creation. All creation is represented by the four elements of Earth, Wind, Fire and Water. Each of the four symbols/elements should be in clear view of the assembly. Earth can be represented by stones and earth with some flowers for colour. Wind can be shown using a fan, while a candle can represent fire. A jug of water and bowl will represent the water element of creation. As each student invokes God's spirit on the different aspects of creation s/he stands behind the element in question.

OPENING PRAYER

God of power and love,
You promised to pour out your spirit on all creation,
Send down the fire of your love
Send down the rain of your love
Send down your Spirit, breathe life into your people and all the earth.
We ask this through our Lord Jesus Christ who lives and reigns with you and the Holy Spirit forever and ever.
Amen.

PRAYER OF PENITENCE

The Spirit comes with the fire of justice. Forgive us for the times we have extinguished that fire by complacency and injustice.

Lord have mercy.
Lord have mercy.

The Spirit comes with the rain of love. Forgive us for the times we have raised the umbrella of hate or indifference.

Christ have mercy.
Christ have mercy.

The Spirit comes with the fresh winds of change. Forgive us for the times when we have resisted and closed the windows to the Spirit's voice.

Lord have mercy.
Lord have mercy.

May Almighty God have mercy on us, forgive us our sins and bring us to everlasting life. Amen.

READING   Acts 2:1–4

INVOCATION OF THE SPIRIT ON THE ELEMENTS OF CREATION

1.   EARTH
                   This we know, the earth does not belong to us, we belong to the earth.
                   All things are connected like the blood that unites one family.
                   We did not weave the web of life, we are merely a strand in it.
                   Whatever we do to the web, we do to ourselves.
                   We give thanks for the gift of creation.
                   Loving God, send your spirit to all creation and strengthen our unity with one another and will all creation.

2.   WIND
                   Great Spirit of God,
                   Blow softly on us all, embrace us always with your warm and gentle breezes.

Whisper soft reminders in our ears of the presence of God.

Caress us with your strength and blow away the cobwebs of sin from our lives.

Loving God, awaken us to the power of your Spirit and bless us with your love.

3.   **FIRE**

Even the smallest spark can become a mighty flame.

Spirit of God, you are the flame of love in our lives.

Forgive us when we douse your flame or ignore the smallest flicker of your love.

Warm our hearts that we might truly live.

Radiate love where it has been dampened.

Send your Spirit, the flame of love, to transform our lives.

4.   **WATER**

Water sustains and gives life. It helps the seed to grow and ensures a rich harvest.

Water quenches our thirst and helps us to grow.

Spirit of God, we watch and wait for the rain of grace into our souls.

Loving God, may your Spirit free us from hatred, greed, fear and our lack of love for your gifts.

Transform us into streams of living water flowing with life, hope and love.

LITANY OF THE HOLY SPIRIT

READER	God of all beginnings
RESPONSE	We worship you.

READER	God of all endings
RESPONSE	We worship you.

READER	God of all we undertake
RESPONSE	We worship you.

READER	Life-loving Spirit
RESPONSE	We worship you.
READER	Breath of the universe,
RESPONSE	We worship you.
READER	Craftsman of the heavens
RESPONSE	We worship you.
READER	Creator of the Earth
RESPONSE	We worship you.
READER	Source of all life,
RESPONSE	We worship you.
READER	Light of our lives
RESPONSE	We worship you.
READER	Strength in our weakness
RESPONSE	We worship you.
READER	Consolation in our grief
RESPONSE	We worship you.
READER	Healer of our wounds
RESPONSE	We worship you.
READER	Shelter in our storms
RESPONSE	We worship you.
READER	Tenderness in our distress
RESPONSE	We worship you.
READER	Giver of joy
RESPONSE	We worship you.
READER	Giver of comfort
RESPONSE	We worship you.
READER	Giver of Peace
RESPONSE	We worship you.

READER	Giver of Wisdom
RESPONSE	We worship you.
READER	Giver of Right Judgment
RESPONSE	We worship you.
READER	Giver of Good Counsel
RESPONSE	We worship you.
READER	Giver of Strength
RESPONSE	We worship you.
READER	Giver of Awe and Wonder
RESPONSE	We worship you.
READER	Giver of Love
RESPONSE	We worship you.
READER	Wellspring of life, Spirit of God Most High
RESPONSE	We worship you.

CLOSING PRAYER

Father of Love,
Help us to hear the good news of our faith.
The Spirit is alive!
Breathe, children of God,
Breathe, the fresh winds of the Spirit.
Taste, children of God,
Taste the quenching waters of God's love.
Touch, children of God,
Touch the heat of God's passion for justice.
Give us this grace through Christ our Lord.
Amen.

THE SACRAMENTS

MOMENTS OF SPECIAL ENCOUNTER WITH CHRIST

Music suggestions can be found in the Appendix

This liturgy could be appropriate if the pupils have been studying the sacraments as part of the catechetical programme. This liturgy will help to reinforce the lessons and the symbols associated with each sacrament.

Items/Symbols you will need:
1. Baptism: jug of water and bowl
2. Confirmation: candle
3. Eucharist: bread/wine/grapes/wheat
4. Reconciliation: purple stole/purple cloth
5. Sacrament of the Sick: jar of oil
6. Marriage: a pair of rings
7. Holy Orders: a Bible

INTRODUCTION

LEADER   As Christians we believe that God watches over us and protects us throughout our lives. We turn to him in prayer for his help when we need it. There are also times in our lives when we approach God for his special help at significant times. These are moments of special meeting with Christ and we call them sacraments. A sacrament is a sacred or holy moment when we meet Christ in a special way. We ask for his help at important times of our lives and he gives us that help to live our Christian lives.

OPENING PRAYER

God our Loving Father, you loved the world so much that you sent your only Son into the world to save us. In the seven sacraments you continue to send us your son to help us in our lives. We thank you for the grace and help you give us through the seven sacraments and we ask you to continue to bless us with your love through Christ our Lord. Amen.

LEADER   We do not make the journey of life alone, but in the company of others. When we travel the Christian life we are united with all those people who share our belief in God and his Son Jesus. We are brought into the Christian family by the Sacraments of Christian Initiation; Baptism, Confirmation and Eucharist. To be Christian means to imitate Jesus by loving all our fellow human beings.

BAPTISM   Before he began preaching and teaching, Jesus was baptised by his cousin John in the Jordan river. At his Baptism, God's voice was heard saying, 'This is my beloved Son, listen to him.' When we were baptised we were welcomed into the Christian family. May this water remind us of our own baptism. When we were washed clean of sin and given a new life close to Jesus.

Student presents jug of water and bowl.

CONFIRMATION   After the resurrection and ascension of Jesus, the apostles were gathered together in one room. Jesus had promised to send them the Holy Spirit. The Holy Spirit came on the apostles in the form of tongues of fire and gave them the courage to tell other people about Jesus, about all he had said and done. The flame of this candle reminds us of the flame of the Holy Spirit that was sent into our hearts at Confirmation. May we always have the courage of the Holy Spirit to live out our religion in our daily lives.

Student presents candle

EUCHARIST	Before Jesus died he shared a last supper with his apostles. He took some bread and said, 'This is my body'. Then he took some wine and said, 'This is my blood'. Then he shared them with his apostles and said, 'Do this in memory of me'. Whenever we celebrate the Mass and receive the Eucharist, Jesus comes into our lives in a special way. May this bread and win remind us that Jesus is very close to us when we open our hearts to receive him.

Student presents bread and wine or grapes and wheat.

LEADER	God is especially close to those who are broken-hearted or vulnerable. Because we are human, we sometimes fall into sin. Because we are frail, we sometimes become ill. Jesus comes to us in a special way in the healing sacraments of reconciliation and the sacrament of the sick.
RECONCILIATION	We try to live good and Christian lives, but sometimes we fall short of the ideal. We do things that harm our relationship with God and with other people. When we are sorry, Jesus comes to us with forgiveness in the sacrament of reconciliation. May this purple stole, which the priest wears when he forgives sins in God's name, remind us of the healing that comes from saying sorry.

Student presents purple stole.

SACRAMENT OF THE SICK	In his ministry, Jesus healed many who were sick. He gave them new hope and new life. When people are weakened by sickness they seek the healing strength that comes from Jesus. In ancient times, oil was used to soothe and heal the wounds of those who suffer. May this oil remind us of the healing that Christ can bring, as we pray for all our fellow Christians who are sick or suffer in any way.

Student presents jar of oil.

LEADER	When we choose a path in life we hope that God will accompany us on our journey. We pray that Jesus will give us guidance in the

choices we make in the vocational sacraments of marriage and holy orders.

MARRIAGE

Jesus revealed his true identity as God for the first time by working the miracle at the wedding of his friends at Cana in Galilee. When two people promise to love and live for each other, all their lives Jesus is part of their dreams and hopes in the sacrament of marriage. May these rings remind us that Jesus is part of every genuine act and promise of love.

Student presents rings.

HOLY ORDERS

Jesus gathered twelve apostles around him to help him in his work. He challenged them to serve all people and to preach the Good News of God's Kingdom to them. May this bible remind us that God calls people to preach the Gospel and serve others. Jesus strengthens them by the sacrament of Holy Orders and sends his Spirit to sustain them in their mission.

Student presents Bible.

CONCLUDING PRAYER

LEADER

Father of all, you renew your spirit within us through the power of the seven sacraments. Keep us always open to that spirit as we journey through life. Fill us with your grace through Christ our Lord. Amen.

A VISIT TO THE CHURCH

Music suggestions can be found in the Appendix

Sometimes we go to the church for liturgy and prayer and do not fully take in the significance of our surroundings. This is an opportunity to look closely at the church and try to understand many of the things we have often seen and sometimes take for granted.

LEADER — Jesus gathered with his disciples to celebrate the first Eucharist in the upper-room in Jerusalem. In the early Christian times they gathered in the homes of believers to celebrate the liturgy. As the numbers of Christians grew they began to come together in larger venues. They were always mindful of the promise of Jesus, 'Wherever two or three gather in my name, there am I among them'. All who came together were part of the Christian family and this was still a home – it is the Church, the house of God.

SACRISTY — We gather in the sacristy. In this room preparations are made for the care of God's house and the celebration of the liturgy. It is here that the ministers prepare and pray before leading God's people in prayer. May we always be mindful of the sacredness of our times of prayer. We ask God to create within us the Spirit that allows us the pray with a sincere heart.

CHURCH — As we enter the church, we are aware of the many people of faith who have come here to deepen their faith and celebrate their relationship with Jesus Christ. Churches come in many shapes and sizes. Some churches are built in the shape of a cross to remind us of the great sacrifice of Jesus Christ. When we gather to pray in this building, we are united with people of every generation throughout the whole world who come to meet their God in a sacred place. May the Lord keep us mindful of our unity with all believers from the greatest cathedral to the smallest chapel and challenge us to reach out in support of fellow Christians who struggle with life.

In medieval times, it was popular for people to go on a pilgrimage to holy sites associated with Jesus. In Jerusalem pilgrims would follow the way that Jesus went carrying his cross. From time to time along the way they would stop and remember the suffering Jesus. Not everybody could take the time or had enough money to go to the Holy Land. The churches set up the stations of the cross so that people could make the pilgrimage in their own communities. As we look at the images of Christ's suffering and death we pray for all who suffer in the world today and as we journey through life may the Lord guide us to work to alleviate the suffering of others.

THE STAINED GLASS WINDOWS

Stained glass windows began to appear in our churches in the eleventh and twelfth centurys. At that time not everybody was able to read so the stained glass windows were used to depict evens from the lives of the saints or from the life of Christ. Parents would use them to teach their children about the great things God had done for his people. Stained glass windows became the poor man's Bible. As we look upon the stained glass windows we pray that we will always be able to share the stories of what Christ has done for us and bring light and colour into darkened lives.

SANCTUARY   The sanctuary is a holy place and in the ancient temple it was the place where the presence of God was believed to reside in a special way. At the heart of our sanctuary is the ALTAR. In ancient times the people would sacrifice some of their crops or flocks as a way of thanking God for his goodness. This sacrifice was made on the altar. In our church, the altar is the place where the priest celebrates the mass and re-enacts the sacrifice that Jesus made on the cross of Calvary. The priest leads the people in prayer from the PRESIDER'S CHAIR. As we stand in this holy place, this sanctuary, we praise God for his closeness to his people and we thank him for the gift of his son.

AMBO   In ancient Greece, an 'ambo' was an elevated place from where important words were spoken. In our church the ambo is the place from which the Word of God is proclaimed. God's message to us comes in his holy word. Let us pray for the grace to hear God's call in his word, that we may keep his commandments and grow in his love.

TABERNACLE   We conclude our visit to this church by coming to pray at the tabernacle. In the early Church the Eucharist was reserved here so that the sick could receive Jesus in their times of trial. The Eucharist is the body, blood, soul and divinity of Jesus Christ truly present in the form of bread and wine. In the tabernacle is the presence of Jesus Christ. Here we can come in prayer as countless generation have done before us. We are mindful that he always listens to sincere prayers. We ask that as we leave this church, this house of God, we may take with us the spirit of Christ's presence wherever we may go.

OUR FATHER

BLESSING

May the Father bless us, for we are his children, born to eternal life. Amen
May the Son show us his saving power, for he died and rose for us. Amen
May the Spirit give us the gift of holiness and lead us by the right path, for he dwells in our hearts. Amen.

LITURGY FOR A RETIRING TEACHER

Scripture texts and music suggestions can be found in the Appendix

This liturgy can be used to honour a retiring teacher. It can be used as part of a Eucharistic Celebration or can be adapted to stand alone. The participants and readers should be drawn from a wide cross-section of the school community and include colleagues from the staff, students, parents, management, the teacher's own family and the wider community.

balance MGR R'ment + all other issues re end of year.

GATHERING RITUAL

PRESIDER	*Celebrate* We gather together to honour a lifetime of service and dedication to the teaching vocation. We rejoice and at and give thanks for the great work that has been done by N. We pray that he/she will enjoy a long and happy retirement.
MANAGEMENT REPRESENTATIVE	We honour N's. commitment to the Catholic ethos of this school. By his/her word and example he/she has given to the students a pride in belonging and a strong sense of the values that this school seeks to promote. *(Present a symbol of the school's ethos)*
TEACHING COLLEAGUE:	We honour N's. dedication to the teaching vocation. By his/her hard work he/she has always striven to achieve the best for his/her students. *(Present symbol of teaching or of a particular subject)*
STUDENT	We honour N's. involvement in extra-curricular activities. By his/her sharing of talents we have all grown as people. *(Present symbol of activities in which teacher was involved)*

PARENT	We honour N's. love for his/her students. By his/her dedication to the welfare of our children he/she has helped our families.
	(Present symbol of family/love)
COMMUNITY REPRESENTATIVE	We honour N's. passion for this community. By his/her concern he/she has enriched our community.
	(Present symbol of local community)
PRESIDER	N., in your career you have touched the lives of countless people. We gather in prayer to give thanks for all that you have achieved and to pray God's blessing on you and your family as you begin your retirement.

OPENING PRAYER

God almighty, giver of all good gifts, we praise you for your goodness. We ask you to bless our teachers who have imparted to our children the wisdom and wonder of your world. Grant a long and happy retirement to N. that he/she may continue to grow in your grace and love. We ask this through Christ our Lord. Amen.

FIRST READING	Ecclesiastes 12:9–13
RESPONSORIAL PSALM	
	Psalm 27
	Response: The Lord is my light and salvation.
SECOND READING	Philippians 1:3–11
GOSPEL	Luke 15:3–7

PRAYERS OF INTERCESSION

PRESIDER   Dear Lord, we celebrate your care, your goodness and your love. We look ahead into all the unknowns and ask you to grant us hearts that are open to your spirit and truth as we place our needs before you.

1.   For the Church that has been enriched by the teaching vocation of N., that it may always be a sign of God's love and an instrument of his peace.

Lord hear us.

2.   For all whose lives have been touched by the teaching of N., that they may grow in knowledge and awareness of being God's beloved children.

Lord hear us.

3.   For our school community, that we may be united in faith and love striving to help build up God's kingdom in our midst.

Lord hear us.

4.   For N. that God may grant him/her a long retirement filled with grace and blessings surrounded by love and care.

Lord hear us.

5.   For all who are denied an education, that God's people may work to promote justice and opportunities for all.

Lord hear us.

6.   For those who have died, that as they lived their Christian vocation in this life, they may live for eternity in the presence of the God they tried to serve.

Lord hear us.

Lord our God, We praise and celebrate your love for us as shown in this gifted and caring teacher. Let his/her example be a model for us all. Grant us the grace to go forth and learn – the greatest gift we can give our teachers in return. We ask all our prayers through Christ our Lord. Amen

PRAYER OVER THE GIFTS

Loving God

Accept the gifts we offer to you in appreciation of all you give and teach us. Make them holy with your blessing that they may become the food for eternal life and we may learn the lessons of your love. We ask this through Christ our Lord. Amen.

POST-COMMUNION REFLECTION

Why God Created Teachers

When God created teachers,
He gave us special friends
To help us understand His world
And truly comprehend
The beauty and the wonder
Of everything we see,
And become a better person
With each discovery.
When God created teachers,
He gave us special guides
To show us ways in which to grow
So we can all decide
How to live and how to do
What's right instead of wrong,
To lead us so that we can lead

And learn how to be strong.
Why God created teachers,
In His wisdom and His grace,
Was to help us learn to make our world
A better, wiser place.

Anon.

CONCLUDING PRAYER

Gracious God, keep us always mindful of your compassion and love and give us the gifts we need to spread your message of love among those we meet. Open our hearts to give us courage that we may share the adventures that the future has to offer. Grant to N. a happy and fulfilled retirement. We ask this through Christ our Lord. Amen

BLESSING

(Invite the assembly to extend their hands in blessing over the retiree)

Send your blessing on this wonderful teacher. Reward him/her for the sacred work of education. Hold him/her in your heart. Refresh them when they tire, comfort them when they despair and magnify their moments of joy and peace. Give new life and hope to all who have learned of your love through their teaching. This blessing we now call down in the name of the Father, Son and Holy Spirit. Amen.

ANTI-RACISM LITURGY

Scripture texts and music suggestions can be found in the Appendix

This might be suitable at the end of a module in the RE programme that examines the morality of racism. A focus for the liturgy could be created using posters/symbols provided by groups like Amnesty International or Trócaire. If there are students in the class from different ethnic groups perhaps they can suggest something to represent their culture. Things that represent slavery, discrimination or exclusion could also be used such as locks, chains, barbed wire etc.

INTRODUCTION

We are becoming familiar with reports on racism from all points of the globe, we are well aware that the urgency is real, we must act together to eradicate this evil that threatens our world. We must meet the obstacles on the way, and though the journey is risky, we must go forward.

The face of racism looks different today than it did in the past. Overt racism is easily condemned, but the sin of racism is often with us in more subtle forms. This day we gather in the love of God and neighbour to examine patterns of racism in our hearts, and our world systems. We beg for both forgiveness and conversion as we open our hearts and minds in prayer.

OPENING PRAYER

Good and gracious God, you invite us to recognise and reverence your divine image and likeness in our neighbour. Enable us to see the reality of racism and free us to challenge and uproot it from our society, our world and ourselves.

We make our prayer through Christ our Lord Amen.

SCRIPTURE READING

READING   Luke 10:25–27

REFLECTION – THE STORY OF ROSA PARKS

(This story could be read by a number of different readers)

Where do we begin to combat racism, and related intolerances? We must begin where we begin every thing we do for the people of God, with ourselves. Individuals can make a profound difference if we have the courage to stand up for justice and right.

On Thursday evening December 1, 1955, after a long day of work as a seamstress for a Montgomery, Alabama, department store, Rosa Parks boarded a city bus to go home. Mrs Parks walked past the first few — mostly empty — rows of seats marked 'Whites Only'. She finally settled for a spot in the middle of the bus. Black people were allowed to sit in this section as long as no white person was standing.

After several more stops the bus was full. The driver noticed that all the seats in the 'Whites Only' section were now taken, and that more white people had just climbed aboard. He ordered the people in Mrs Parks's row to move to the back of the bus, they all got up . . . except for Rosa Parks.

Rosa Parks finally had enough of being treated as a second-class citizen. When she didn't move, the driver left the bus and returned with a policeman. Mrs Parks was promptly arrested for violating segregation laws.

Knowing that the city bus system depended heavily on the African-American community, the black leaders agreed to call a boycott of all city buses on Monday, December 5. A new and popular minister in Montgomery by the name of Martin Luther King Jr. was chosen to lead the boycott. United in protest, boycotters chose instead to walk, take carpools, pedal bicycles, and even ride mules to get to work instead of boarding the buses.

Slowly but surely the bus company began to lose money — 75 per cent of its customers were black. Nevertheless, the company didn't change its segregation policies. Angry and frustrated, some of the white people of Montgomery began to harass and threaten anyone involved with the boycott. The protesters continued to follow the guidance of their leader, Dr King, using non-violent tactics no matter how much they were provoked

Finally, almost one year after Rosa Parks's refusal to give up her seat, the Supreme Court ruled — on November 13, 1956 — that Montgomery's segregation laws were unconstitutional.

Although the boycott wouldn't have been successful without the unified effort of Montgomery's 17,000 African Americans, no one will ever forget Rosa Parks, the brave woman who led the way.

The very next day, Rosa Parks and Martin Luther King, Jr., boarded a city bus. Proudly, Rosa Parks took a seat right up front.

PROFESSION OF FAITH & COMMITMENT TO COMBAT RACISM

(This should be copied and distributed to all so that students can recite it together.)

We believe in one God
Who created the world,
Who will unite all things in Christ.
We believe in God the Son,
Who became human: died and rose in triumph
To reconcile all creation to God;
To break down every separating barrier
Of race, culture or class,
And to unite all people into one body.
We believe in God the Spirit,
The pledge of God's kingdom
Who gives the Church power to proclaim the good news to all the world,
To love and serve people,
To strive for justice and peace:

To warn that God judges both the individual and the nations;
And to summon all the world to accept God's kingdom, here and now.

We pledge to examine our own biases and positions and earnestly work to resolve them.

We pledge to live by compassion and be consciously inclusive of all individuals.

We pledge to affirm the value of diversity.

We pledge to promote understanding, inclusion, and mutual respect and build community within all races, and cultures.

We pledge to advocate for justice, demand equal opportunity for all and so help create a beloved community for everyone to share.

CLOSING PRAYER:

Good and gracious God,

Who loves and delights in all people, we stand in awe before You, knowing that the spark of life within each person on earth is the spark of your divine life. Be merciful and compassionate as we try to combat the evils of this life; rejection, intolerance, discrimination. God of Mercy, help us to see the best within ourselves, so that we may see the best in all persons. Give us the vision to see You in all humanity, so wonderfully created by You. May all peoples live in Peace. Amen.

BLESSING

Now let us go in peace and faith and be witness to hope and God's Healing Grace and may the Spirit of God go with us. May the knowledge of God's faith and trust in us abide within us. May knowledge of God's Love support us in whatever we have to do to combat racism throughout our Community and the world.

Amen

APPENDIX

MUSIC

RESOURCES

(G&P) *Glory & Praise* series

(IC) *In Caelo – songs for a pilgrim people,* edited by Liam Lawton (Veritas, ISBN: 1 85390 466X)

(MSS 2003) Maynooth Summer School 2003

(S our F) *Sing Our Faith*

CHECKLIST

Many of the liturgies included in this book have an overlap with those presented in *Liturgies for Post-Primary Schools,* and the musical suggestions in this volume include some of our 'older' liturgical music. I am aware that not all Religion Departments have a huge supply of music books, so I have tried to keep the resource list as short as possible. Make friends with your local Choir Director, who I am sure would be only delighted to help you access music.

1.   Once music has been chosen:

     a.   Check the key of the piece, especially if students are being asked to sing along with a CD. The atmosphere can be ruined by a piece being sung too low or too high.

     b.   Not all verses are necessarily suitable to the liturgy at hand. Select the verses carefully beforehand.

     c.   Make sure copies of the words are available for everyone.

2.   The use of instrumental music can be very powerful during liturgies – there is a huge amount of suitable traditional music available, especially many beautiful slow airs that fit well with reconciliation services, offertory processions, Easter liturgies, and so on. Even a solo tin whistle works well in this context.

3. The use of classical music should not be avoided, especially if music students are present. A piece with a definite melody usually works best. Try using some CDs featuring instrumental solos, for example, David Agnew's *Into the Mist*, which features solo oboe.

4. If you find Taizé chants are favourably received, try some Gregorian chant.

MUSIC SUGGESTIONS TO ACCOMPANY LITURGIES.

1. **OPENING YEAR MASS**
    All are welcome, Marty Haugen, (IC)
    Thanks be to God, Stephen Dean, (IC)
    One Bread we break, Stephen Dean, (MSS 2003)
    Sing O Sing, Dan Schutte, (G&P 3)

2. **OPENING YEAR MASS FOR EXAMS**
    Take and Eat, Michael Joncas, (S our F)
    You are Mine, David Haas, (IC)
    With a Shepherd Care, James J. Chepponis, (S our F)
    Where your treasure is, Marty Haugen, (MSS 2003)
    Light of Christ, Carey Landry, (G & P 2)

3. **PRAYER SERVICE FOR TEACHERS**
    Deep within, David Haas, (GIA Publications)
    Set your heart on the higher gifts, Stephen C. Warner, (IC)

4. **HARVEST THANKSGIVING**
    O Joyful Light, Michael Joncas, (G & P 2)
    Taste and See, James E. Moore, (S our F)
    In the Lord I will be ever thankful, Taizé, (S our F)

5. **ALL SAINTS**
    I will be the vine, Liam Lawton, (IC)
    The Summons, Kelvin Grove, (S our F)
    Go out and tell the Good News, Laura & David Ashe, (MSS 2003)

6. **SERVICE OF REMEMBRANCE**
Instrumental music or Traditional slow airs would be appropriate.
To You o Lord, Michael Joncas, (G & P 2)
Jesus, remember me, Taizé, (S our F)
Psalm 23, ad. Marty Haugen, (IC)
In memory of Jesus, Carey Landry, (G & P 2)

7. **ADVENT RECONCILIATION**
Save us O Lord, Bob Dufford, S.J., (G & P 3)
Turn to me, John Foley S.J., (G & P 3)
Nada te turbe, Taizé, (S our F)
Eagle's Wings, Michael Joncas, (S our F)
You are mine, David Haas, (IC)

8. **VOICES OF CHRISTMAS**
Let Heaven Rejoice, Bob Dufford S.J., (G & P 2)
Wake from your sleep, Dan Schutte, (G & P 3)
The maiden and her child, Liam Lawton, (GIA Publications)
Night of Silence, Daniel Kantor, (S our F)
(written to be sung simultaneously with Silent Night)
The Sacred Child, Micheal O'Suilleabhain, (IC)
Prepare the Way of the Lord, Taizé, (G & P 1)

9. **INTERFAITH DIALOGUE**
You raise me up, Brian Kennedy
Prayer of Peace, David Haas, (S our F)
Peace Prayer, John Foley S.J., (G & P 2)
In faith, in hope, Christopher Walker, (MSS 2003)
All people that on earth do dwell, (IC)

10. **PRAYER FOR PEACE**
May God Bless Us, Ephraim Feeley, (IC)
Servant Song, Rory Cooney, (G&P 3)
You are mine, David Haas, (S our F)
My Soul in stillness waits, Marty Haugen, (S our F)

11.   **OUR FATHER**
        Amen Siakudamisa, S. African Trad, (S our F)
        We praise you, Balhoff, Ducote, Diagle, (G & P 3)
        I will rejoice, Grayson Warren Brown, (G & P 2)
        Theoraigh me, a Thiarna, S. S. Wesley, (MSS 2003)
        Any arrangement of the 'Our Father' from mass settings could also be used

12.   **LENTEN RECONCILIATION**
        Return to God, Marty Haugen, (S our F)
        Somebody is knocking at your door, Marty Haugen, (S our F)
        Abba Father, Carey Landry, (G&P 1)
        Prepare the way of the Lord (canon), (G&P 1)

13.   **WAY OF THE CROSS**
        Be Still, David J. Evens, (IC)
        Only this I want, Dan Schutte
        O,comfort my people, Text based on Isaiah 40, (IC)
        (Traditional Irish melody)
        Your Song of love, Robert Fabing S.J., (G&P 3)
        A huge amount of Taizé music is suitable for this liturgy.

14.   **THE PASSION**
        Jesus, remember me, Taizé, (S our F)
        Magnificat, Taizé, (S our F)
        What wondrous love is this, Alexander Means, (S our F)
        O Sacred Head, text: M. Farrell, (IC)
        Wait for the Lord, Taizé, (IC)

15.   **PENTECOST**
        Tar Anuas, A Spioraid, Ite O'Donovan, (IC)
        Christ, Your footsteps through the desert, Stuempfle/Ebenezer, (MSS 2003)
        Dust and Ashes, David Haas, (S our F)
        Send us Your spirit, Dan Schutte, (G&P 3)

16.   **SACRAMENTS**

Only a Shadow, Carey Landry, (G & P 2)

17.   **VISIT TO CHURCH**

We love this place, Christopher Walker, (IC)

This alone, Tim Manion, (G & P 3)

All are welcome, Marty Haugen, (S our F)

Gather, Liam Lawton, (IC)

Watch and Pray, Taizé, (G & P 3)

18.   **RETIRING TEACHER**

Take O take me as I am, John Bell, (S our F)

Teach me your ways, Michel Guimont, (S our F)

To you O Lord, Michael Joncas, (S our F)

19.   **ANTI-RACISM**

Though the mountains may fall, Dan Schutte, (G & P 3)

In the stillness of the night, Daigle, Ducote, (G & P 2)

Love one another, Bob Dufford, S.J., (G & P 2)

Jesu, Jesu, Tom Colvin, (S our F)

This is my will, James Quinn, (IC)

Where is the Love, Black Eyed Peas

One bread, one body, John Foley S.J., (G & P 2)

SCRIPTURE READINGS

1.

OPENING OF THE SCHOOL YEAR

LITURGY FOR FIRST YEAR STUDENTS

Philippians 4:4–9

Rejoice in the Lord always; again I will say, Rejoice. Let your gentleness be known to everyone. The Lord is near. Do not worry about anything, but in everything by prayer and supplication with thanksgiving let our requests be made known to God. And the peace of God, which surpasses all understanding, will guard your hearts and your minds in Christ Jesus.

Finally, beloved, whatever is true, whatever is honourable, whatever is just, whatever is pure, whatever is pleasing, whatever is commendable, if there is any excellence and if there is anything worthy of praise, think about these things. Keep on doing the things that you have learned and received and heard and seen in me, and the God of peace will be with you.

Psalm 34

Response: I will bless the Lord at all times.

I will bless the Lord at all times;
his praise shall continually be in my mouth.
My soul makes its boasts in the Lord;
let the humble hear and be glad.

I sought the Lord, and he answered me,
and delivered me from all my fears.
Look to him, and be radiant;
so your faces shall never be ashamed.

This poor soul cried, and was heard by the Lord
and was saved from every trouble.
The angel of the Lord encamps around those who fear him,
and delivers them.

Mark 4:35–41

On that day, when evening had come, he said to them, 'Let us go across to the other side.' And leaving the crowd behind, they took him with them in the boat, just as he was. Other boats were with him. A great windstorm arose, and the waves beat into the boat, so that the boat was already being swamped. But he was in the stern, asleep on the cushion; and they woke him up and said to him, 'Teacher, do you not care that we are perishing?' He woke up and rebuked the wind, and said to the sea, 'Peace! Be still!' Then the wind ceased, and there was a dead calm. He said to them, 'Why are you afraid? Have you still no faith?' And they were filled with great awe and said to one another. 'Who then is is this, that even the wind and the sea obey him?'

2. **OPENING OF THE SCHOOL YEAR**

LITURGY FOR EXAM CLASSES

Isaiah 55:6–9

Seek the Lord while he may be found, call upon him while he is near; let the wicked forsake their way, and the unrighteous their thoughts; let them return to the Lord, that he may have mercy on them, and to our God, for he will abundantly pardon. For my thoughts are not your thoughts, nor are your ways my ways, says the Lord. For as the heavens are higher than the earth, so are my ways higher than your ways, and my thoughts than your thoughts.

Psalm 20

Response: The Lord answers in the day of trouble.

The Lord answer you in the day of trouble!
The name of the God of Jacob protect you!
May he send you help from the sanctuary,
and give you support from Zion.

May he grant you your heart's desire,
and fulfil all your plans.
May we shout for joy over your victory,
and in the name of our God set up our banners.
May the Lord fulfil all your petitions.

Now I know that the Lord will help his anointed;
he will answer him from his holy heaven
with might victories by his right hand.

Luke 11:9–3

'So I say to you, Ask, and it will be given you; search, and you will find; knock, and the door will be opened for you. For everyone who asks receives, and everyone who searches finds, and for everyone who knocks, the door will be opened. Is there anyone among you who, if your child asks for a fish, will give a snake instead of a fish? Or if the child asks for an egg, will give a scorpion? If you then, who are evil, know how to give good gifts to your children, how much more will the heavenly Father give the Holy Spirit to those who ask him!

3.   **A SERVICE OF PRAYER FOR TEACHERS**

Matthew 5:14–16

'You are the light of the world. A city built on a hill cannot be hid. No one after lighting a lamp puts it uner the bushel basket, but on the lampstand, and it gives light to all in the house. In the same way, let your light shine before others, so that they may see your good works and give glory to your Father in heaven.'

4.   **A SERVICE OF HARVEST THANKSGIVING**

Deuteronomy 26:1–4

When you have come into the land that the Lord your God is giving you as an inheritance to possess, and you possess it, and settle in it, you shall take some of the first of all the fruit of the ground, which you harvest from the land that the Lord your God is giving you, and you shall put it in a basket and go to the place that the Lord your God will choose as a dwelling for his name. You shall go to the priest who is in office at that time, and say to him, 'Today I declare to the Lord your God that I have come into the land that the Lord swore to our ancestors to give us.' When the priest takes the basket from your hand and sets it down before the altar of the Lord your God.

5.   **FEAST OF ALL SAINTS – HEROES OF FAITH**

John 11:25–26

Jesus said to Martha, 'I am the resurrection and the life. Those who believe in me, even though they die, will live, and everyone who lives and believes in me will never die. Do you believe this?'

6.   **A SERVICE OF REMEMBRANCE**

Lamentations 3:17–24

My soul is bereft of peace;
I have forgotten what happiness is;
so I say, 'Gone is my glory,
and all that I had hoped for from the Lord.'

The thought of my affliction and my homelessness
is wormwood and gall!
My soul continually thinks of it
and is bowed down within me.
But this I call to mind,
and therefore I have hope.

The steadfast love of the Lord never ceases,
his mercies never come to an end;
they are new every morning;
great is your faithfulness.

'The Lord is my portion', says my soul,
'therefore I will hope in him.'

Psalm 23

Response: The Lord is my shepherd, there is nothing I shall want.

The Lord is my shepherd, I shall not want.
He makes me lie down in green pastures;
He leads me beside still waters;
He restores my soul.
He leads me in right paths
for his name's sake

Even though I walk through the darkest valley,
I fear no evil;
for you are with me;

your rod and your staff –
they comfort me.
You prepare a table before me
in the presence of my enemies;
you anoint my head with oil;
my cup overflows.

Surely, goodness and mercy shall follow me
all the days of my life,
and I shall dwell in the house of the Lord
my whole life long.

John 14:1–7

'Do not let your hearts be troubled. Believe in God, believe also in me. In my Father's house, there are many dwelling places. If it were not so, would I have told you that I go to prepare a place for you? And if I go and prepare a place for you, I will come again and will take you to myself, so that where I am, there you may be also. And you know the way to the place where I am going.' Thomas said to him, 'Lord, we do not know where you are going. How can we know the way?' Jesus said to him, 'I am the way, and the truth, and the life. No one comes to the Father except through me. If you know me, you will know my Father also. From now on you do know him and have seen him.'

7. **ADVENT SERVICE OF RECONCILIATION**

John 3:14–21

And just as Moses lifted up the serpent in the wilderness, so must the Son of Man be lifted up, that whoever believes in him may have eternal life.

'For God so loved the world that he gave his only Son, so that everyone who believes in him may not perish but may have eternal life.

'Indeed, God did not send the Son into the world to condemn the world, but in order that the world might be saved through him. Those who believe in him are not condemned already, because they have not believed in the name of the only Son of God. And this is the judgement, that the light has come into the world, and people loved darkness rather than light because their deeds were evil. For all who do evil hate the light and do not come to the light, so that their deeds may not be exposed. But those who do what is true come to the light, so that it may be clearly seen that their deeds have been done in God.'

10. **PRAYER FOR PEACE**

Isaiah 2:4

He shall judge between the nations, and shall arbitrate for many peoples; they shall beat their swords into ploughshares, and their spears into pruning hooks; nation shall not lift up sword against nation, neither shall they learn war any more.

Psalm 95:1–2;3–5

Response: The Lord judges the people with fairness.

But the Lord sits enthroned forever,
He has established his throng for judgement.
He judges the world with righteousness;
He judges the peoples with equity.

The Lord is a stronghold for the oppressed,
a stronghold in times of trouble.
And those who know your name put their trust in you,
for you, O Lord, have not forsaken those who seek you

Sing praises to the Lord, who dwells in Zion.
Declare his deeds among the peoples.
For he who avenges blood is mindful of them;
he does not forget the cry of the afflicted.

John 14:27–29

Jesus said to his disciples, 'Peace I leave with you; my peace I give to you. I do not give to you as the world give. Do not let your hearts be troubled, and do not let them be afraid. You heard me say to you, 'I am going away, and I am coming to you.' If you loved me, you would rejoice that I am going to the Father, because the Father is greater than I. And now I have told you this before if occurs, so that when it does occur, you may believe.

12.   LENTEN RECONCILIATION SERVICE

Joel 2:12–14a

Yet even now, says the Lord,
return to me will all your heart,
with fasting, with weeping, and with mourning;
rend your hearts and not your clothing.
Return to the Lord, your God,
for he is gracious and merciful,
slow to anger, and abounding in steadfast love,
and relents from punishing.
Who knows whether he will not turn and relent,
and leave a blessing behind him.

15. **PENTECOST**

Acts 2:1–4

When the day of Pentecost had come, they were all together in one place. And suddenly from heaven there came a sound like the rush of a violent wind, and it filled the entire house where they were sitting. Divided tongues, as of fire, appeared among them, and a tongue rested on each of them. All of them were filled with the Holy Spirit and began to speak in other languages, as the Spirit gave them ability.

18. **LITURGY FOR A RETIRING TEACHER**

Ecclesiastes 12:9–13

Besides being wise, the Teacher also taught the people knowledge, weighing and studying and arranging many proverbs. The Teacher sought to find pleasing words, and he wrote words of truth plainly.

The sayings of the wise are like goads, and like nails firmly fixed are the collected sayings that are given by one shepherd. Of anything beyond these, my child, beware. Of making many books there is no end, and much study is weariness of the flesh.

The end of the matter; all has been heard. Fear God, and keep his commandments; for that is the whole duty of everyone. For God will bring every deed into judgment, including every secret thing, whether good or evil.

Psalm 27

Response: The Lord is my light and salvation

The Lord is my light and my salvation
Whom shall I fear?
The Lord is the stronghold of my life,
Of whom shall I be afraid?

One thing I ask of the Lord
That will I seek after:
To live in the house of the Lord
All the days of my life.
To behold the beauty of the Lord
And to inquire in his temple.

Philippians 1:3–11

A Reading from the letter of St Paul to the Philippians.

I thank God every time I remember you, constantly praying with joy in every one of my prayers for all of you, because of your sharing in the gospel from the first day until now. I am confident of this, that the one who began a good work among you will bring it to completion by the day of Jesus Christ. It is right for me to think this way about all of you, because you hold me in your heart, for all of your share in God's grace with me, both in my imprisonment and in the defense and confirmation of the gospel. For God is my witness, how I long for all of you with the compassion of Christ Jesus. And this is my prayer, that your love may overflow more and more with knowledge and full insight to help you to determine what is best, so that in the day of Christ you may be pure and blameless, having produced the harvest of righteousness that comes through Jesus Christ for the glory and praise of God.

Luke 15:3–7

So he told them this parable: 'Which one of you, having a hundred sheep and losing one of them, does not leave the ninety-nine in the wilderness and go after the one that is lost until he finds it? When he has found it, he lays it on his shoulders and rejoices. And when he comes home, he calls together his friends and neighbours, saying to them, 'Rejoice with me, for I have found my sheep that was lost.' Just so, I tell you, there will be more joy in heaven over one sinner who repents than over ninety-nine righteous persons who need no repentance.

19.   **ANTI-RACISM LITURGY**

Luke 10:25–27

Just then a lawyer stood up to test Jesus 'Teacher', he said, 'what must I do to inherit eternal life?' He said to him, 'What is written in the law? What do you read there?' He answered, 'You shall love the Lord your God with all your heart, and with all your soul, and with all your strength, and with all your mind; and your neighbour as yourself.' And he said to him, 'You have given the right answer; do this, and you will live.'